S0-BLM-964

WHAT MEN ARE ASKING

What Men Are Asking

SOME CURRENT QUESTIONS IN RELIGION

HENRY SLOANE COFFIN

THE COLE LECTURES FOR 1933
DELIVERED AT VANDERBILT UNIVERSITY

Essay Index Reprint Series

BOOKS FOR LIBRARIES PRESS
FREEPORT, NEW YORK

Reprinted 1970 by arrangement with Abingdon Press

INTERNATIONAL STANDARD BOOK NUMBER:
0-8369-1791-X

LIBRARY OF CONGRESS CATALOG CARD NUMBER:
70-117770

PRINTED IN THE UNITED STATES OF AMERICA

TO THE MEMORY

OF ONE OF THE EARLIEST COLE LECTURERS

CHARLES CUTHBERT HALL

IN HONOR, AFFECTION, AND GRATITUDE

Alii laboraverunt: et vos in labores eorum introistis

PREFACE

IN SENDING THESE LECTURES TO THE PRESS I should like to express my gratitude to the members of the Faculty of Vanderbilt University, to the students and ministers in the School of Religion, and to the Nashville audiences who accorded them so sympathetic a hearing. I am also indebted to several of my long-suffering colleagues—to Professor John Baillie for an addition to Lecture III, to Professor J. E. Frame who read over Lecture IV, to Professor Reinhold Niebuhr who offered some criticisms on Lecture VI, and especially to Professor Henry P. Van Dusen who read the entire manuscript and made a number of clarifying suggestions.

H. S. C.

Union Theological Seminary,
New York City,
June, 1933.

CONTENTS

I

WHERE CAN WE START?

"WHERE CAN WE START IN OUR RELIGIOUS thinking to-day, when the bottom has dropped out of all that we used to consider solid?" It was a middle-aged professional man who put the question. "There were certain things which we took for granted, and proceeded to build on them; but all our assumptions are gone, and there is no foundation left on which to begin."

Many thoughtful people in the decade and a half since the Great War have shared this bewilderment. The basis on which their spiritual life was thought to rest disappeared.

In this country a generation ago, when our questioner was at school and college, an individual here and there doubted the existence of a God who had personal dealings with men. But such skeptics were a small minority in the community, and were regarded as "peculiar" by their neighbors. In the rural district where the present speaker began his ministry as a divinity student six and thirty years ago, the local blacksmith, a follower of Robert Ingersoll, was spoken of, almost with dread, as an infidel. Edmund Gosse tells an amusing incident of finding himself in a crowded London bus with Rossetti, when the latter, feeling uncomfortably packed in, loudly announced that he was an atheist; whereupon a number of the passengers left the bus.[1] One could hardly procure a seat in a New York subway to-day by this means.

Many thousands among us, in all walks of life, assume that the Deity of Biblical religion does not exist. Some of them are militant in their attack on Theistic faith, not only because they think it false, but also because they believe that it hinders man's growth to reliant maturity and retards moral progress. Others consider religion an escape from reality—

> "a shadow isle of bliss
> 'Midmost the beating of the steely sea."

Or they regard it as a survival of childish credulity, to be dealt with gently as adults handle an imaginative child's faith in fairies, or to be laughed at as a weakness that should be outgrown. In any case they do not treat it seriously, for it will disappear with advancing knowledge, or, should it persist, it will be classed as the delusion of a maladjusted mind.

A generation ago the few who questioned the existence of God were usually confident that man is a noble creature with almost limitless possibilities. If they did

[1] See references beginning on page 189

not affirm, "I believe in God, the Father almighty, Maker of heaven and earth," they believed in man, increasingly mighty, progressively maker of a better earth. A romantic confidence in man underlay European and American thought throughout the Nineteenth Century. Walt Whitman chanted for both continents his exuberant credo in the capacities of plain people: "What an india-rubber principle there is, after all, in humanity." [2] In this faith our country set out to provide educational opportunities for everybody, and our colleges flung wide their doors to all comers. We envisioned a land of sages.

To-day an admired writer (Cabell) calls man "a parasite infesting the epidermis of a midge among the planets." [3] The Great War appalled us with the helplessness of man to control his own inventions humanely, and with the brutality of human nature. The difficulties which the world has experienced since in adjusting its economic problems has shaken our self-assurance. We have become aware how susceptible men in masses are to suggestion. Newspaper proprietors, political managers, advertising experts, amusement purveyors, have assumed that our minds are machines which can be worked fairly simply. Feed them the appropriate propaganda and the desired result will be forthcoming. A popular psychology which regards us as bundles of stimulus-and-response bonds is in part an attempt to rationalize the prevalent distrust. The soul has followed God into the discard.

A generation ago the public was overwhelmingly optimistic. An editorial in a religious newspaper declared:

> "The world is a pretty good institution. God said he thought so, and most men agree with him." [4]

About the same date Kipling made one of his characters, who had knocked about the globe, conclude his observations:

> Gawd bless this world! Whatever she 'ath done—
> Excep' when awful long—I've found it good.
> So write before I die, 'E liked it all! [5]

Unbelievers in any God were as satisfied with life. Henley wrote:

> Life is worth living
> Through every grain of it
> From the foundation
> To the last edge
> Of the corner-stone death.[6]

And not only did men find the world good, but it seemed to them palpably getting better. It did not need to be remade; it had resident forces that promised an ever brighter future. The discoveries of scientists, the devices of inventors, the organizing skill of business men, the increasing good will of supposedly kindly folk, would usher in an age unmarred by poverty or disease or strife. Progress was inherent in the fabric of the cosmos. A minor poet voiced the dominant feeling:

> Thus, I muse, at the core
> Of our battered old planet,
> Something young and untainted,
> Something gay and undaunted,
> Like a bud in its whiteness,
> Like a bird in its joy
> Pushes steadily forward—
> Singing.

But so-called "muckrakers" began showing up our vaunted institutions. A new race of biographers tore the haloes from the brows of saints. Novelists exposed Main Street and Zenith City. The drama presented sordid and ignoble people working out their semi-animal destinies. Strident voices of revolt were heard everywhere, but they were not hopeful voices. A book of the present season grants that "this world of ours is interesting," but offers "an embarrassing profusion of almost equally unsatisfactory possibilities."[7] If we were intoxicated a few years back by our achievements, we are as bewildered to-day by our impotence and futility.

A generation ago it was assumed by almost everyone in our Western world that life was an education for a larger existence beyond our bourne of time and space. Browning, perhaps the poet most prized by the more thoughtful of that day, rang the changes on "man learningly lives" and has "forever"[8] in which to continue the process. Edward Rowland Sill, whose verse had a wide vogue in the nineties because it voiced the mood of the more spiritually-minded, wrote:

So shall it be, that, when I stand
On that next planet's ruddy-shimmering strand,
I shall not seem a pert and forward child
Seeking to dabble in abstruser lore
With alphabet unlearned, who in disgrace
Returns, upon his primer yet to pore—
But those examiners, all wise and mild,
Shall gently lead me to my place,
As one who faithfully did trace
These simpler earthly records o'er and o'er.[9]

To-day most people are not aware of living in a schoolroom, because the larger world for which they are being trained has dropped below the rim of consciousness. Dr. George A. Gordon, in one of my last conversations with him, contrasted the difference in this respect between his people in the Old South Church, Boston, at the outset and at the close of his forty years' ministry. At the end of the nineteenth century in dying they had an anticipation of a glorious life into which they were to enter, while two decades later, still nominally believing in immortality, they had no definite or inviting hope in prospect.

Many of our finer spirits view life as a chance to invest themselves for a better society to-morrow. They frequently denounce the craving for personal survival as conceited and selfish: why should any man think himself indispensable to the universe? To be sure they have moments when they would give anything to rejoin those whom they have lost, or, like Thomas Huxley, they wish they might count on an occasional return to see how affairs are going in this interesting world. Perhaps it is the grip which earth's ongoings have on men's interest, as well as the fading out of the traditional pictures of heaven, which has obliterated the prospect from life's spiritual horizon. We seldom think of one another as immortal beings, and while our education may gradually be reordered to train students as citizens of a more socialized commonwealth, one sees few Christian institutions of learning deliberately planning their curricula to prepare them for the eternal city of God.

A generation ago, whether one shared or not the religious faith of Jesus, it was almost universally believed that his ethical principles, such as the Golden Rule and the permanent monogamous family, were self-evident. A rare objector, like Samuel Butler, might protest that in social advance "Jesus Christ's carriage blocks the way"; but few cared for social advance along Butler's lines. His biographer records this note of his:

> "There will be no comfortable and safe development of our social arrangements—I mean we shall not get infanticide, and the permission of suicide, nor cheap and easy divorce—till Jesus Christ's ghost has been laid." [10]

To-day cheap and easy divorce is certainly available, and while the specter of Jesus still stalks the earth, many regard his teaching as futile sentimentality, or as irrelevant to present conditions, or lump it with the static factors which uphold the present outworn social order.

However we may account for it, the years since the War have been a relatively irreligious period. The spectacle of Christians butchering fellow-Christians inevitably raised the question of the value of the faith both professed. A recent book on contemporary Britain by Professor Dibelius of Berlin, in its chapter on "England After the War," declares that "for the first time in its history, it would seem as though England had broken with Christianity." [11] At our side of the Atlantic, Professor Montague of Columbia, in a lecture delivered at Yale, uses almost identical words:[12]

> "For perhaps the first time in history we are confronted with the prospect of a complete secularization of the opinions, the practices, and the emotions of mankind."

Similarly Professor Ortega of Madrid, discussing the danger to civilization from "the mass-man" as he calls him, who knows no other method of altering conditions than violence, ascribes the peril to the obliteration of his soul.[13]

Not only has Soviet Russia done its utmost to suppress both Christianity and Judaism, but Turkey has abolished the Caliphate and set itself to banish Mohammedanism and all other religions from its schools.

Christianity does not confront rival faiths on mission fields, but both at home and abroad it faces the secular mind.

This mind is dominant on the campus of our own universities. In many institutions with Christian origins and charters no serious attempt is made by the faculty to present the religious life to the students. Corporate worship, in which the whole body of professors and students join, has been abandoned. A chapel is maintained, where a chaplain, with the aid of a handful of earnest members of the faculty and with the occasional patronage of the administrative officers, carries on services attended by a small fraction of the students. If courses in religion are offered in the curriculum, the attempt is made to keep the approach to the subject strictly objective, and any effort so to present it as to enlist devotees is severely frowned on as "unacademic." The instructor may profess no religious loyalty. One wonders whether the English department would intrust the course in Wordsworth to a professor who was not a devoteė of the poet and eager to kindle in his class a like appreciation. The attitude toward Christianity on the part of many of our college faculties is akin to that of an early French Academician, Butrau, who surprised his friends one day by lifting his hat to a crucifix as he passed in the street. "Ah, then," they remarked, "you are on better terms with

God than we supposed?" "On bowing terms," came the reply; "we don't speak." [14]

The situation in the world and in our own universities is reflected within the Church. Ministers and people feel themselves on the defensive. Instead of inviting the public to services where they are led to pray and listen to the living God, "discussion groups" are organized, where people are encouraged to talk about religion. Instead of boldly pushing their propaganda of the gospel, they make "surveys" of their work. An earlier generation surveyed the wondrous cross, and confidently proceeded to direct the eyes of the world to the Crucified, sure that such a look at him would bring life. Instead of being vibrantly aware of God, and of his infinite resources, contemporary Christians are self-conscious, examining their own "religious experience."

Much of this experience might be labeled "vestibule religion." Sermon after sermon is preached to show that Christian faith is not incompatible with current science or philosophy or psychology, and that it is possible to be both a believer and intellectually respectable. Suppose such sermons effected their purpose, their hearers would be no further in the sanctuary than the lobby. Indeed many who speak on religion seem hardly inside the front door. They point to the temple of faith as an ancient historic building still standing and worthy of serious investigation. There is far too little testimony from within to the richness of the life with

Christ. And the curious, looking from the outside, question whether the foundations have not been so shaken that the old walls will presently crack. Even the believing within are panicky, and seem comforted when an occasional distinguished physicist or biologist trusts himself with them in the worship of God.

An insecure home is detrimental to all members of the family. A group of brothers and sisters meeting to discuss whether their parents were reliable, and whether they could be called loving, would indicate a parlous state of domestic affairs. A wholesome family never thinks of itself, much less talks about the mutual relations of its members. They take for granted and rejoice in one another, and living together strengthen one another for life's demands. Their home, steadfast in its abiding loyalties, is the unquestioned foundation of their lives. A healthy Church is not thinking of itself, nor discussing whether prayer is possible, or whether its God can have personal relations with his children. It lives with him, hears him, waits on him, and is wise and strong in his fatherly fellowship. It does not speak of "religion"—the relationship between the Divine and believers—any more than husband and wife talk of their relation. It bears witness to the life with Christ in God, and uses its vital energy in the Father's business.

One would not be unsympathetic with this questioning both inside and outside the Church. Who can be, remembering his own infirmities? And periods of doubt, when all assumptions are challenged, have often been precursors of ages of vigorous faith.

> On life's broad plain the ploughman's conquering share
> Upturned the fallow lands of truth anew.

The questioning is a sign of wistfulness. It is something to be interested in religion; but it is still a long way short of being alive unto God. One would like to take people's attention away from themselves, for after so much talk about "religious experience," it is time to cease looking in and to look out and up. There is a current revolt from subjectivism in both music and art. Men have been too preoccupied with themselves—their moods and emotions, their reactions to mountains and sunsets and to their mates. There is a similar turning from subjectivism in religion. In Protestant Europe a vital movement is attempting to face man with a transcendent Deity, the altogether Other than himself. In Britain few thinkers have more influence than the late Baron von Hügel, who stressed the "given" elements in religion, and spoke of God as "the healing Divine Dwarfer of our poor little man-centered, indeed even self-centered, schemes." [15]

Admittedly there is no way in which we can climb out of ourselves, and apart from our feelings and minds attain a disclosure of reality which we can proclaim wholly objective. Our physical scientists are reminding us that their knowledge of the material universe is mediated through the impressions which it makes upon their intellects, and that their descriptions of it are symbolic representations of how it seems to them. If God reveals himself to men, he can do so only through their perception of his presence in nature or in historic events or in to-day's suggestions and happenings which move them. If, then, we look out and up, this is no claim that we leave ourselves behind. It is still *we* who look, and *we* who report what we see; but our look is not self-centered nor confined to man, but attempts to embrace the total impression of reality.

Where, then (to answer the query with which we began), can we start in our religious thinking to-day? If one is looking for an accessible God, and if, as our predecessors assure us, God is looking for us, a man ought to start just where he is. Men, being different in themselves and differently circumstanced, will take various points of departure; and there are numberless roads—intellectual, æsthetic, moral, mystical—by which they tell us they are found of God. But for such a questioner as we have instanced we may call attention to two commonplaces, indisputably true, which, if we examine their obvious implications, take us to the bottommost fact in life, and afford us the sense of touching its solid foundation.

The first of these overlooked commonplaces is the general agreement among decent folk that, when one does anything well, he ought not to credit it wholly to himself; and that, when one does anything badly, he should not altogether excuse himself. We instinctively dislike both the man who ascribes his achievements to his own prowess, and the man who shifts the blame for his failures to other shoulders or saddles them upon circumstances. This is not to encourage morbid self-depreciation which underestimates one's power or over-stresses one's guilt. But we assume that a man's accomplishments are not entirely his own, and that his misdoings should be acknowledged as mainly his own. We are repelled from anyone who gives the impression of satisfaction with his attainments, and from anyone who dodges his responsibility for mistakes. We praise the successful, but we think it becoming in him to deprecate our praise as not his due. We censure the ill-doer, and we think less of him if he attempts to evade his full share of the condemnation.

This is a firmly rooted assumption which governs our estimates of our fellow men. It may be called unreasonable—a survival in us of some primitive superstition. The fact remains that we do not like to associate with the complacent who attribute their well-being to their own abilities, nor with the impenitent who assign their non-successes to bad luck. It is both good manners and good morals to receive successes thankfully and in blunders and failures to hold ourselves guilty.

A feeling so widely and so deeply embedded in human

beings must have behind it a long experience. It must be a response which man has found himself compelled to make to the total effect of existence upon him. It appears to imply that man cannot help recognizing in this puzzling world a factor that works for his welfare, so that if things go well with him, he must not be unmindful of it, or even if they are adverse, he inclines to believe their very hardness means kindly by him. And if life goes wrong with him, he must charge this in large part to his own folly or weakness. This is the religious response to life—a response of thankfulness and penitence. It is the response which alone seems to produce likable men and women. Without these qualities of gratitude for a goodness to them beyond their desert, and of contrition for their own faultiness, men and women are not agreeable members of human society.

It is worth noticing how these qualities persist in those who have lost the religious convictions on which they rest. One who sixty years ago felt the full force of the difficulties to faith and parted with Christianity, Leslie Stephen, when his wife died, began a sentence in a letter to Lowell: "I thank"—then recollecting that he had none to whom he could think himself indebted for the dear companion of his heart, and for his affection for her, he wrote: "I thank—something—that I loved her as heartily as I know how to love." [16]

In our own day, a brilliant young English novelist,

Katherine Mansfield, compelled for health's sake to seek a home in Switzerland, finds herself rejoicing in the tonic mountain air and the loveliness of the forest in summer, and, writing to a friend, concludes her description of her surroundings:

> "If only one could make some small grasshoppery sound of praise to *someone*—thanks to *someone*. But who?" [17]

And in a different mood she tells another correspondent:

> "God is now gone for all of us. Yet we must believe; and not only that—we must carry our weakness, and our sin, and our devilishness to somebody." [18]

And she suggests that love between lovers must take the place of the religious relationship, but suddenly breaks off in dissatisfaction: "But oh, it is no good."

Here are persons with the religious response to life, although they have lost religious faith; and their thankfulness and penitence render them very attractive. They are qualities which enhance their social value.

The impression which the universe makes on us through beauty, or truth, or human goodness, is, of course, not the only impression. There are contradictory impressions of the indifference or cruelty of nature, of the tragedy of human relations, of the baffling mystery of existence; but this gracious aspect remains a haunting impression to be reckoned with. It has come so repeatedly to mankind that the responsive pattern of gratitude and humility has been formed in them and appears in the finest of them. Take one of the most charming and lovable figures in English literature, Charles Lamb, with an insane sister who had murdered her mother, and with an unsympathetic and exacting father, and doomed himself to uncongenial clerical work for long hours. We find him writing to Coleridge:

> "I am starving at the India House, near seven o'clock without my dinner, and so it has been and will be almost all the week. I get home at night o'erwearied, quite faint —and then to *cards* with my father, who will not let me enjoy a meal in peace—but I must conform to my situation, and I hope I am, for the most part, not unthankful." [19]

There is a man lifted out of as dark and trying a situation as can be imagined by the dominant impression which life makes upon him, despite its other impressions. One may call him deluded when he says: "I hope I am, for the most part, not unthankful." But it is difficult to disparage such a man or belittle that in him which raises him triumphantly over prostrating circumstances. His thankfulness aids him to keep his sanity, to discharge his duties, to be a devoted brother and friend, and the writer of essays and letters which are refreshing springs to this day. In his grateful response to life there is something of highest worth to society.

Is this response, persisting singularly in some who have parted with religious faith, and producing in both believer and unbeliever unquestionably valuable results in character, without foundation? What an anomaly that would make it in a world where all organisms adapt themselves to environing fact! Or are these folk, so gracious in their humility and thankfulness, the products of a gracious Being, with whom, whether they can name him or not, their sensitive souls are in correspondence? Is the intuition which renders them likable men and women an hallucination? Or is it an adjustment which man at his sanest makes to reality?

The other commonplace which may serve to steady us, and to start us on a similar line of spiritual discovery, is the fact that amid our present confusions a vast amount of goodness still remains indisputably good. While some traditional religious and ethical conceptions are questionable, the staple virtues are as valuable as ever. It is still good to seek after knowledge and not be ignorant, still good to speak the truth and hate lies, still good to be honest and not a scamp, still good to be chaste and not lecherous, still good to face life with courage and not run away from difficulties, still good to be self-controlled and not the thrall of moods or appetites or circumstances, still good to be generous in thought and act, still good to be public-spirited, and concerned for the weal of society, still good to cultivate things lovely and avoid adding to the ugliness of the world, still good to be thoughtful, kindly, modest. The standard virtues have not declined in value. There has been no slump in the moral market.

It is still good for a man and woman who marry to stay married. The post-war novelist Katherine Mansfield, who certainly cannot be accused of conventional religious bias, writing to another novelist, Sylvia Lynd, says:

"What is happening to 'modern pairs'? They are almost extinct. I confess, for my part, I believe in marriage. It seems to me the only possible relation that really is satisfying. And how else is one to have peace of mind and do one's work? To know *one other* seems to me a far greater adventure than to be on kissing acquaintance with dear knows how many. It certainly takes a lifetime, and it's far more 'wonderful' as time goes on. . . . People nowadays seem to live in such confusion. . . . I wish you'd write a novel about married happiness. It is time for one." [20]

That keenly analytical mind, viewing life with a novelist's objectivity, found marriage as a settled institution the only foundation for her own emotional stability and for freedom to do her work.

When the papal encyclical on marriage was issued in January, 1931, an apt comment appeared in a journal where one might not expect ethical criticism—the *New Yorker*. Remarking that the Pope had said everything about marriage except the most significant thing (which might be due, the writer suggested, to His Holiness' lack of experience), he continued:

"What Pope Pius seems to us to have missed completely about Christian marriage was this: that, with all its falling from grace, it is still a lot of fun; more fun than practically any other form of institutionalized living, so much fun in fact, that almost everyone still believes in it pretty thoroughly, even the most violent reformers and renovators."

There is a writer familiar with life in a social stratum where divorce is extremely common, justly criticizing an ecclesiastic for attempting to bolster a Christian institution with many props, and failing to set forth the inherent goodness of the institution itself.

And as for the Golden Rule, where is it being intelligently tried and found unsatisfactory? When one looks at the dealings of man with man, of nation with nation, of race with race, and discovers aught to commend and rejoice over, is it not an instance where the law of love is being practised?

When men speak of the foundations as being destroyed, by all means let us not urge them to look within and study their own religious experiences. That only serves to render them more self-conscious. What they need is to be aware of something outside themselves which upholds and steadies them. Bid them go on being righteous. There are things which they know to be good: they cannot fool themselves into calling them bad. They may not be able to explain why they are good. Why certain musical compositions charm us, we can never wholly tell. But we cannot help responding to them and finding them entrancing. Goethe assured us that beauty can never understand itself. Why certain persons attach our devotion remains only partly explicable. But there are men and women who grapple us to themselves with hoops of steel. Similarly our consciences confront imperatives—things we ought to do, things we must do. Here is that which is "given," to use von Hügel's word.

On Captain Scott's last expedition to the Antarctic, he and two companions set out on a final dash to the Pole. One of these companions, an officer in the Dragoons, Captain Oates, finding himself exhausted and with one foot so swollen and constantly frost-bitten that he could not hope to go on, in order to spare his companions any further trouble with him said to them, "Well, I am just going outside, and I may be sometime," [21] and walked out of their tent into the blizzard and was seen no more. That was calm self-sacrifice, with no applauding public, prompted by something to which he bowed as supreme. We cannot withhold our admiration. His act was heroically good. Courage, loyalty, self-control, love are good—good for us and good for all men.

And when a bewildered man, faithful to them, resolutely obeys his conscience, he knows himself a soul, no automaton as his detractors assert. Some of his moral judgments may be unenlightened and require revision. But responding to such conscience as he possesses, he knows that he is more than a mechanism worked by stimuli. He can highly resolve. He stands over against the physical universe with its power to slay him, over against his fellow-mortals exerting social pressure upon him, over against the impeding elements within himself. There is somewhat higher which commands his allegiance. This which constrains, taking a Captain Oates to his death to save his comrades—call it Duty, call it Love—is compelling. It is an ultimate from which there is no appeal. We touch that which is basic in existence. It is as real as life and death, and more cogent than life, sending that gallant officer out to die. "I can do no other."

And then, almost inevitably, a man adds: "So help me God." For why should Duty be supreme with him? Why does not a Captain Oates, flinging himself away in the Antarctic blizzard, seem to us a fool? The physical universe does not care for heroism. The blizzard freezes the righteous as ruthlessly as the unrighteous. Fellow-mortals are not at once responsive to truth. Prophets are usually unrecognized by contemporaries who acclaim some showy demagogue. The righteous himself is often shrouded in clouds and darkness, when he wonders whether he may not be mistaken. Luther, whose memorable utterance at the Diet has just been quoted, breaks off in the midst of a passionate prayer: "My God, art thou dead?" [22] His Master on the cross felt the foundations had slipped from under him: "My God, why hast thou forsaken me?"

But it is in such experiences when, despite destroyed foundations, the righteous continues in his righteousness, that his soul, broad awake, reaches up and discovers God. Why are duty, truth, love compelling? They exist outside himself and belong in the fabric of the universe. The soul in him which answers to them gropes for a kindred Soul at the heart of the cosmos. Every sustaining foundation smashed, faith steps forth on the seeming void and finds rock beneath. "So help me God."

The good which grips a righteous man, patently good for him and for his fellows, must be part of a vaster Good, above both him and them. Neither he nor they have decided that fidelity, honesty, justice, courage are good. These lay compelling hands on consciences generation after generation. Think again of that determined figure going out into the Antarctic storm to die. Call such an ideal of devotion the survival of a tribal taboo. Why does such a taboo survive? Is it merely a casual product flung up by the evolutionary process with no more relation to the central stream of the ongoing universe than a wisp of foam which a running brook leaves about a stone? If it were that only, could it persistently hold the uttermost loyalty of men? Is it not related to something central in the universe itself? Is it not the main stream—the Spirit over all, through all, in all?

Starting with two obvious commonplaces—that men are not counted desirable members of society who plume themselves on their merits or excuse their defects, and that there are duties which men are impelled to aver good for themselves and good for others—we have dug down to basic reality. There are times when men cannot help being thankful, and times when they face an all-but-irresistible obligation. Here they confront ultimate spiritual fact. They may interpret variously that to which they are grateful, and that which imperiously grips their conscience: but here is the foundation of existence. Religion interprets it as the living God.

Let us instance the supreme religious Interpreter. Jesus once sketched a picture of the test which the weather of our stormy planet applies to housebuilders. One builder had taken for granted that the surface soil was solid and had set his house on that, another had digged deep until he reached rock and started his building on that. Unconsciously he was giving us a chapter of autobiography. All about him folk erected their lives and based their society on the beliefs and ideals of their time. They seemed to him tragically insecure. For himself he digged deep, and went far beneath current creeds and standards, and was convinced that love is the ultimate base of the universe—the very nature of God. It was to a Self-giving Father that he owned himself indebted for his all, and to that Father's purpose of goodwill toward his children that he gave his all. In such faith and love he founded his house—the spiritual home he was rearing for his brethren. The cosmic weather showed him no favors. He did not expect that it would. It was part of his realistic outlook that the sun shines on evil and good, and rains fall on just and unjust. This did not disturb his deeper insight that over all is a God of love. To him he was thankful, to him he was dedicated.

The test of the cosmic weather came for him. Rains descended, floods came, winds blew. Did ever habitation of souls undergo severer strain than Golgotha? His opponents were confident that he and his cause were destroyed. His followers thought that he had misjudged foundations and that his house had collapsed. "We hoped," they said ruefully. He himself at the height of the storm could not feel beneath him the upholding rock. But history has justified him. His house has stood, and has become with succeeding generations the spiritual home of more and more of his grateful and devoted brethren.

The same cosmic weather recurs, and the house of his faith, which subsequent generations adapt for the dwelling of their spirits, is exposed to similar tests. In their adaptations of it, Christians unwittingly remove it from the foundation on which Jesus set it.

This had happened again in our time and caused the necessity of rebuilding implied in the question with which we began. Dr. Wingfield Stratford, the historian of British civilization, in an appraisal of the nineteenth century, pays tribute to "the God's plenty of individual character" by which that age was distinguished, and lauds the idealism, the faith, the humanitarian achievement of a notable period. But he points out the factors, already apparent in the nineties, which in the next decade brought on the Great War, and speaks of "the downfall of that edifice which our fathers wrought so nobly *in all but the foundations*." [23] Their ideals of economic justice, their standards of international obligations, their conceptions of God were inadequate. While morally earnest, the ethics and religion of the period were not commensurate with the development of society on other lines. The structures of their business, their politics, their religion, were shaking before the century closed, and the present generation has seen them crash.

James Truslow Adams arrives at a similar estimate of that period in this country, particularly of the post-war decade when, tired of idealism, we placed our destinies "in the hands of safe realists, hard-headed business men who would stand no nonsense about 'moral issues.' " [24] He reminds us that these "practical men" bankrupted both our idealism and our prosperity. Our characteristic American philosophy, Pragmatism, fails to satisfy because it furnishes us with no standard by which to determine whether anything "works" or not. Instead of measuring the life of a man or a nation by the abundance of things which he produces or possesses, our need is to ask what manner of man or of nation is produced. This swift survey of the American scene brings up the same issue—on what spiritual basis are we rearing the edifices of our education, our industry, our public policy?

And this suggests why (to revert to the language of our questioner) the bottom seems to drop out of that which has been deemed solid. Every generation must have fresh insights, or rather a freshening of an old and continuing revelation, to keep itself established on the living God. For Christians that revelation is found in Jesus Christ. To the question, "Where can we start in our religious thinking?" we answer: "Start with him."

The structure of our thought must be our own, and into its building will go all the knowledge of our time; but its inspiration throughout must be from him, and his mind must dominate and be apparent everywhere. This is not to cramp our age in the forms of a remote past. When an orchestra to-day renders the works of a classic composer—a Bach or a Palestrina—it does not reproduce the music as it was originally given. The instruments in the hands of our musicians are different from those available two or three centuries ago. This requires some rearrangement of the parts. Nor can musical productions be precisely duplicated. They are interpreted and re-created each time they are given. But the score of the composer with his melodies and harmonies animates and governs the current rendering.

We, with the instruments of our time—our communities, our nation, our world, ourselves—must re-create those airs and rhythms and chords heard long since in Galilee and Jerusalem, and heard again and again through the subsequent centuries. It must be *our* arrangement and *our* interpretation. But it will be the music of Christ's faith and love. And that (to employ an ancient metaphor) is the music of the spheres—the measures to which the worlds and the generations move, as they utter the mind of God.

—⊰ II ⊱—

OF WHAT USE IS RELIGION?

WE WERE DEALING IN THE LAST LECTURE with a questioneer who was interested in and eager for religious faith. To many to-day such faith seems not only irrational but also irrelevant. At a New England college, during a series of meetings on the subject of religion where opportunity was offered for personal interviews with the speaker, a student came into the room with the remark: "I don't know why I am coming to you; I haven't any particular difficulty for which I'm seeking help. God does not interest me enough to raise difficulties. My question is: Of what use is religion anyhow?"

It is a common question in this practical age, and it betrays a point of view from which one is not likely to see very far into religion. For God is not a utility. Friendship will not open its door to the man who keeps asking of acquaintances: "Of what service can this man be to me?" He who attempts to use friends ruins friendship. Marriage will not afford access to its riches to him who asks, "Of what advantage will a wife be to me?" and proceeds on that basis to propose to a suitable young woman. He who uses a wife degrades marriage. Any man who approaches the holiest relation of all—his fellowship with the Most High God—expecting to use the Lord of heaven and earth for his purposes debars himself from communion with the Father of his spirit.

To be sure friends often prove of greatest service, and a wife is a quite incalculable enrichment; but their uses are by-products of a companionship in which friend and wife are prized for their own sakes, and not as conveniences. God is of the utmost service to all his children, whether they are aware of him or not, and those who know him call him their chief treasure; but he is never sought and found by those who look for his uses to them. He is not a force, like steam or electricity or radio-waves, to be studied and harnessed for our ends. He is not a lackey waiting to be summoned to render us some assistance, "a cosmic bell-hop," or a Prospero's Ariel. That is magic, not religion. God is One who has personal relations with us, and can only reveal himself to those who respond to his trust and love with like faith and devotion.

The student who put the question was, however, high-minded and conscientious, with an eager desire for the triumph of lofty social ideals, and the question meant: "Of what use to these is religion?"

One had to make clear that some forms of religion obviously were of no use to these social purposes, and might be hindrances to them. The religion of Korean peasants is a demon-worship, and fills their minds with fears. They are forever outwitting or placating some hostile spirit only to discover others as malign on their trail. Their religion is a terror from which the Christian missionary with his message of one God, and this God a loving Father, is a welcome deliverance. From which, too, the irreligious scientific education introduced by the Japanese schools is also a deliverance. The fatalistic religion of many Mohammedans proves a barrier to the introduction of measures of public hygiene for their communities. If it is Allah's will that pestilence should come, and that this man and that should die of it, it is not to be withstood. One does not wonder that the rulers of modern Turkey wish to bar religion from its schools.

Certain forms of Christianity have encouraged a similar attitude. A novel of a few years ago describes a settlement of Scandinavian immigrants in Minnesota whose grain was attacked by a blight known as "red rust" [1]—the title of the story. These devout folk took it as a visitation of God. But one bolder and more skeptical young man, Matts Swenson, set himself to produce a blight-resisting wheat; and by procuring other varieties of seed and by crossing their plants with the wheat of the settlers he succeeded. Religion in that community was at this point a foe to its economic well-being. By no means all religion is helpful to our highest social idealism.

But we are not concerned with religion in general but with New Testament Christianity interpreted by the light of the living Spirit in the thought of our time. One could point out that much of the social idealism in the heart and conscience of the student who had asked our question was traceable to this ancestral faith. Even so the question was wrongly worded. Religion is not to be viewed as the servant of social idealism. God is not to be called upon to help "put over" our social program. He is himself more than the most exalted commonwealth of which we dream, where economic and intellectual and æsthetic goods are fully shared. If a man asks religion to aid him in achieving his social goal, that goal stands first with him and God holds a subordinate and auxiliary place in his regard. To be truly religious he must ask, "What is God's purpose for society?" and embrace that purpose because it is God's and therefore promises the utmost human well-being.

Religion is not something useful to be measured by the various services which it performs. Religion of the right sort provides the fertile soil in which economic and intellectual and æsthetic harvests are grown. And even an inadequate or outmoded religion, which is thrown aside, survives in a fervor devoted to other ends. It has been claimed that Holy Russia has not disappeared in Soviet atheism, nor has Jewish piety been lost in the many godless members of that race who fling themselves into a materialistic socialism or communism. Their religion flames in the ardor with which they embrace their new purposes. History reveals that epochs of earnest faith have often been harbingers of advances in material comforts, or of forward strides in culture and discovery, or of a renaissance in the arts. But never has God been sought and found by men who were seeking him for the sake of these results. The whole heart has been centered on him whom to know is life eternal.

But to go back to our student's question, it is well to begin to answer such a query by suggesting that life be viewed with religion entirely banished from the picture. Suppose there be no spiritual interpretation of the universe, what is the outlook?

The human race finds itself on a planet, which like all other planets must run through its life-history of youth, middle age, old age, and death. Sir James Jeans, in a newspaper article, has written:

"The general impression produced by recent investigations is that of a universe slowly but inexorably dissolving into intangible radiation. . . . The earth is a more permanent structure; it may be annihilated by some unknown accident; but not by the mere passage of time; it is endowed with a melancholy immortality which will keep it in existence after light, heat, and life have departed from it, and after the stars have dissolved like the baseless fabric of a vision."

Even should our remote descendants contrive an emigration to another planet, when earth has ceased to be habitable, in a dissolving universe the story of our race is an episode with an inevitable terminus. We may be proud of man's powers to master his physical environment, but these powers are limited, and against a universe in dissolution it is difficult to imagine what the most resourceful could devise. And if the human enterprise be viewed as a casual occurrence in the history of the physical cosmos, it loses the sublime significance with which it has been clothed as the goal and explanation of this world's long evolution. Its existence must be thought of against the background of

Infinite æons ere our kind began;
Infinite æons after the last man
  Has joined the mammoth in earth's tomb and womb.[2]

This prospect has not been easily accepted by social idealists. In our time few have more deserved that name than Beatrice Webb. In her autobiographical sketch, *My Apprenticeship*, she tells us—

"I cannot help having a half-conscious conviction, that, if the human race is mortal, if its existence is without aim, if that existence is to end, at however remote a period, in a complete dissolution, then life indeed is not worth living to the mass of mankind." [3]

Others have settled down to it with apparent satisfaction, and have calmly looked at themselves and their fellow-mortals in this new light. Mrs. Bertrand Russell, in her plea for *The Right to Be Happy*, describes a human being as "a certain kind of conglomeration of processes and chemical reactions which in relation to stimuli and environment produce certain instincts and desires." And she insists:

> "Animals we are and animals we remain, and the path to our regeneration and happiness, if there be such a path, lies through our animal nature." [4]

On a huge scale contemporary Russia is attempting to base a happy national life on a non-religious foundation. There is no denying the admirable devotion of many Communists to their ideal, and the faith, enthusiasm, and sacrifice with which they toil for it. Nor dare we belittle the amazing results achieved along certain lines. But lauded Soviet novelists allow an occasional character to utter the protest of the spiritual man. In his story *Three Pairs of Silk Stockings*, Romanof makes his Arkady confide to his friend Kisliakof:

> "I have just been reading, and thought how unused we have become to having our own thoughts. We are afraid nowadays of admitting the truth to ourselves. We shall soon be quite empty. We are ceasing to believe in the importance and even in the existence of ourselves as units, because everything around us exists in mass form which

has no inner substance whatever. . . . We . . . who still keep intact in the midst of this noisy current, must unite in a sort of church, so as to preserve *our* truth, the truth, common to all humanity, through this epoch, and save it from destruction. . . . I believe that the soul of man, meeting the eternal truth, feels this truth in spite of everything. Nothing can kill this. . . . We must realize that there are times when man loses his inner spirituality, and all that remains is the external, the animal and the mechanical power and capacities, and within—nothing. But I believe that soon man will realize with great anguish that pettiness of external things, and will return to his forgotten soul." [5]

Nevertheless the fact that we do not like the non-spiritual interpretation of the universe and of ourselves is no argument against its truth. We are on our guard against wishful thinking. If this be the true description of the cosmos and of mankind, we must embrace it, however regretfully. There are still duties that remain. We can give ourselves whole-heartedly to making life as tolerable and pleasant for our generation as we can, and to starting our successors with fewer of our recognized handicaps. There is a nobility in adjusting to disagreeable facts, and carrying on by the finest standards so far discovered. But how small a thing man's existence now seems! how lonely is our race with its heart and conscience in an uncaring universe! how meaningless the whole story of its aspirations and struggles until the final curtain is rung down in this vast theatre without spectators to remember any incident in the play!

One cannot assert that with such an outlook social idealism will run dry. There are high-minded folk living on this meager hope. But homesick souls, reared in the household of faith, will unquestionably find their spirits parched in a wilderness with a horizon of futility. We are familiar enough with the experience of individuals who have lost their religious belief. John Addington Symonds, the historian of the Italian Renaissance, in such a mood, penned a letter in which he confessed:

> "How can a man who has not made up his mind about the world and immortality, who seeks and cannot find God, care for politics for instance? He is aimless in life. He has no *point d'appui,* no root, but sprawls, lying like an uprooted plant which belongs to nothing, can attach itself to nothing, and gapes for any chance drop of rain to moisten its fast withering suckers. The longer this skepticism continues, the deeper becomes the unrest, the more worthless appear common sources of interest, the more vacant becomes the soul." [6]

Others have managed to give themselves to immediate tasks with enthusiasm, and have filled their skylines with compassable hopes. But to-day such spirits are living on the impetus of a believing past; and it remains a question whether their idealism is transmissible through several generations. And it is a larger question whether mankind as a whole can keep up its social *morale* and maintain its conscience on a philosophy which robs human existence of ultimate meaning.

In a recent class at Yale a student committed suicide. His father, a well-known man of letters and a poet, was asked by newspaper reporters whether he could account for his boy's act. He told them:

> "My son saw no reason in life, and so none for it. All of us to-day do not know what the reason for life is. We do not understand life. Anyone who pretends to is bluffing. What we want now in place of religious faith is faith in life itself."

But that is a false antithesis. The religious interpretation supplies faith in life. Both our science and our religion make two assumptions—that our world is intelligible and that it is worth knowing. That is the unconscious faith of every scientific investigator. Religion makes it explicit in its conviction that behind and in the world is a wise and good God.

By way of positive answer, then, to the student's question with which we set out, we can say that true religion supplies an explanation of life which illumines it with a glorious purpose for ourselves and for all men. Recall the familiar Christian explanation. Over and in this universe, its Creator and Controller, is a Christ-like Father. His purpose is a commonwealth of sons and daughters akin to him in character, mastering its resources and employing them in brotherhood. Man, his child, is undeveloped and sinful, tragically blind to his true end and often willfully false to his known best, but capable with God's grace of achieving his divine destiny. And God is always, as at Calvary, spending himself for man's redemption, having revealed himself to discerning souls, and supremely in his Word made flesh in Jesus, and ever imparting himself in his Spirit to those who trust him. Life is a redemptive education in fellowship with him and with one another, and such fellowship is eternal, and opens before us endless vistas.

Such in briefest, and obviously incomplete, outline is the Christian faith. It is an explanation of human existence which furnishes two essentials for wholesome living—security and stimulus. It provides us with both a home and horizon: we dwell in God and are sharers of his eternal purpose. It is an interpretation which fits the social ideals cherished by such students as our questioner. Indeed this faith was doubtless one parent of his social idealism. If the faith be ungrounded, that idealism is a half orphan. Programs of economic fellowship and of racial and international brotherhood may be projected without religious faith, but they are thus denied the recognition of their ancestry. They sprang from a religious source, and they only attain their finest development when they remain at home. The Christian interpretation of life both fits our highest social ideals, and keeps constantly toning them up to a yet finer standard. This is not to say that we use God to justify our social hope; but that he is the light by which we see them and see a universe in which they can be achieved.

And true religion not only supplies this interpretation of life, but it also supplies the power by which such life may be lived. God is force as well as light, and force at its highest level is love.

There are three factors with which every man must reckon—the universe, fellow-mortals, and himself. All three are to him both friend and foe.

This world in which we find ourselves is a queer place. Those most at home in it still know it strange. We may call it a schoolroom, but it is a harsh schoolroom. We rejoice in its loveliness, are dependent on its bounty, find it stored with supplies for all save our extremest needs. But it is a threatening place constantly putting us in jeopardy of illness, accident, death. It is a school where there are two curricula to be learned simultaneously: one is the curriculum in which we acquire mastery of the physical forces about us, the other is the curriculum in which we learn to succumb to them and still not let them master us. We have both to transform and to transcend the world.

True religion insists that the world is ours to control. The first pages of the Bible teach man's dominion over the creatures, and its climax presents the lordly figure of Jesus, unafraid of stormy seas, bringing health to disordered minds and bodies, and confident that all man's physical needs are divinely provided for in God's wisely ordered creation. His apostle is sure that the world is ours. It is ours to understand—that is the impetus of science. It is ours to use—that is the impetus of practical undertakings in engineering, in agriculture, in manufacture. It is ours to enjoy—that is the impetus of art, in which we both appreciate the beauty of the world as it is, and create out of its forms and colors and sounds more loveliness.

And not only does religion declare that the world is ours to control, but it dedicates us to control it for the well-being of the whole family of God. It transforms all callings into holy ministries—science into a service of mankind with knowledge, industry into a supply of its wants with goods, art into a satisfaction of its soul with beauty. It frees a man from personal acquisitiveness and commits him to employ whatever he controls in knowledge or wealth or skill for the commonweal of the race.

An instance of this religious devotion to the mastery of nature is the struggle of Sir Ronald Ross at Bangalore to discover the protozoön which is the carrier of malaria. Working in the laboratory and hospital, he wrote:

> I pace and pace, and think and think, and take
> The fever'd hands, and note down all I see,
> That some dim distant light may haply break.
>
> The painful faces ask, Can we not cure?
> We answer, No, not yet; we seek the laws.
> O God, reveal through all this thing obscure
> The unseen, small, but million-murdering cause.

Several years later, he writes in grateful triumph:

This day relenting God
   Hath placed within my hand
A wondrous thing; and God
   Be praised. At His command,

Seeking His secret deeds
   With tears and toiling breath,
I find thy cunning seeds,
   O million-murdering Death.

I know this little thing
   A myriad men will save.
O Death, where is thy sting?
   Thy victory, O Grave? [7]

It is a major tragedy that an otherworldly piety, misrepresenting the faith of Jesus by placing soul and body, the spiritual and the physical in conflict, has made many modern men identify religion with the effort to escape from the world, rather than see in it a stimulus to master the world. For the sake of their social programs they espouse a scientific materialism, and fancy devotion to economic interests the gateway to human welfare and happiness. A religion which does not make its followers concerned for the physical conditions of man's life and enlist them to battle against every preventable cause of human suffering is false to the faith of Jesus.

But the world is never completely ours: it baffles our knowledge and eludes our mastery. Nor does it supply our deepest necessities. We have not only to subdue it and make it serve us, but we have also to rise above it. We know that we owe much to nature as it is. A Wordsworth asserts that he finds in it his supreme inspiration. But it has been well remarked that Wordsworth would have felt differently, had he been living either in the tropics or in the Arctic regions, instead of in the Lake District of temperate England. Religion which draws its inspiration from above the physical world enables men to conquer nature. A Shackleton in the Antarctic or a Stanley in Central Africa find their faith in God a reënforcement in their struggles with an unfavorable environment. Shackleton has written of his sense of the Divine Comrade as he made his way across the barren wastes of ice: "At times the feeling was so strong with me that I would turn, expecting to find a phantom person by my side." [8] Stanley has testified to the power of prayer not only to keep all his faculties alert to cope with the myriad difficulties and dangers of his expeditions, but also to lift him hopefully over hundreds of miles of forest tracks, "eager to face the day's perils and fatigues." [9]

And when failure awaits a man's attempts to understand and dominate the forces about him, his spirit has gone up to God for patience and courage and unconquerable hope. Clement of Alexandria summed up this sense of reinvigoration which comes to baffled men by their faith in Christ in his exquisite testimony: "He has changed sunset into sunrise." [10]

At length the physical universe, to which we belong

through our bodies, gains its ineluctable victory. Death claims our beloved, and there arrives, as George Meredith worded it, after his wife's death,

> The last blank hour of the rack,
> When struck the dividing knife;
> When the hand that never had failed
> In its pressure to mine hung slack.

Or death claims ourselves, and we face the ultimate mystery. Christian faith has its triumph, over this last enemy. Aristides, a philosopher turned disciple, writing about 125 A.D. explains to the pagan public of his day the new confidence concerning the dead in Christ:

"And if any righteous man among them passes from the world, they rejoice and offer thanks to God; and they escort his body as if he were setting out from one place to another near." [11]

In our modern day, the novelist, Charlotte Brontë, when one of her sisters, the brilliant and darling Emily, had died of tuberculosis, and the youngest sister, Ann, was slowly sinking, said in a letter:

"We saw Emily torn from the midst of us when our hearts clung to her with intense attachment, and when loving each other as we did—well it seemed as if (might we but have been spared to each other) we could have found complete happiness in our mutual society and affection. She was scarcely buried when Ann's health failed, and we were warned that consumption had found another victim in her.

I have learned that we are not to find solace in our own strength: we must seek it in God's omnipotence. Fortitude is good, but fortitude itself must be shaken under us, to teach us how weak we are." [12]

Christian faith is both world-transforming, sending us out to master every hostile physical factor to make earth as friendly a place as possible to human beings, and world-transcending, enabling us to go down, as go down we must in this struggle, confident of a yet friendlier place prepared for us in the Father's many-mansioned house.

Fellow-mortals (the second factor) are at the same time assets and liabilities. We cannot estimate what we owe to the groups to which we belong—the family, the church, the community, the nation, the race. Society through its various institutions molds and trains and enriches us. Social pressure holds us up to certain standards of decency, honesty, courtesy. We are born dependent on the care of others for our very life, and it would be difficult to conjecture what our minds would be, had we not been nourished by home and school, by the circle of our friends and the household of faith in which we were reared.

But there comes a point in every man's development when his group becomes his temptation. Social pressure levels down as well as levels up. There were three crosses at Calvary. On two of them were hung men who had fallen below standards prescribed by the community; on the central cross, as the chief offender, hung One who had been far in advance of those standards. He was indebted to his home and synagogue and people; but he discovered that as he grew in moral stature his foes were they of his own household. He heard in the voice of one of his spiritually most congenial friends the seducing Tempter.

Leaders of mankind are always lonely. They must pioneer by themselves.

> Lonely is the man who understands:
> Lonely is vision that leads a man away
> From the pasture lands,
> From the furrows of corn and brown loads of hay
> To the mountain side,
> To the high places where contemplation brings
> All his adventurings.[13]

These lines are put by John Drinkwater in the mouths of the two Chroniclers who comment on the career of Abraham Lincoln, immediately after the scene where, having been notified of his nomination to the presidency, and facing the prospect of attempting to hold together a dividing nation, he falls on his knees in prayer. In the isolation of grave responsibility men have been driven to religion. Instinctively they have looked up. Drinkwater's interpretation of Lincoln is borne out by those impromptu words which came from his lips when, as he left Springfield for Washington to be inaugurated, and his fellow-townsmen gathered at the station to see him off on a perilous journey, he spoke to them from the rear platform of the train:

> "I now leave, not knowing when or whether ever I may return, with a task before me greater than that which rested upon Washington. Without the assistance of that Divine Being who ever attended him, I cannot succeed. With that assistance I cannot fail." [14]

Lincoln was not a conventionally religious man, and his turning to God in his hour of strain reveals the need he felt for more than human assistance to meet the pressure.

A British contemporary of his furnishes another instance of the support to be found in God against the apathy or hostility of one's fellows. Perhaps no man did more for social advance in his generation in Nineteenth-Century England than the Earl of Shaftesbury. His diaries are full of his struggles with his contemporaries in government, in the Church, in the press, and of his recourse to God to uphold him in his humane efforts. Here is a typical entry when he is pleading for legislation to safeguard the wretched children of eight, nine, and ten years, who were forced in danger of suffocation to scramble up and clean crooked chimneys:

> "Very sad and low about the loss of the Sweeps' Bill. The Collar and Garter (which he had been offered) might have choked me. I have not, at least, this or any other government favor against me as a set-off to their insolence and oppression. I must persevere, and by God's help so I will." [15]

Thirteen years later, when he had won protection for the Sweeps, only to discover equally appalling conditions surrounding women and children in factories, and was trying to induce Parliament to enact what seem to us very moderate measures for their protection, is another entry:

"The work to be done is greater than ever: more zeal, more energy, more knowledge, more patience, more activity, more strength, and last, though not least, more money. All this drains one's mind and exhausts one's body, and the simple issue is that many think me a fool, and some regard me as a hypocrite. . . . But surely this career has been ordained to me by God, and I therein rejoice, yea, and will rejoice." [16]

Man at his highest finds himself isolated. He stretches out his hand for comradeship, and feels empty space at his fingertips. Then he reaches up, and is steadied and encouraged by the clasp of the hand of God.

The third, and by far the most difficult factor with which a man must reckon is himself. His personality is his chief tool for effecting his purposes. Qualities in himself account for his successes and his failures. Very largely he makes his own heaven or hell.

And a man's self is such a conglomeration of the divine and the diabolical! Every psychology has its account of what a man is, and of how he has become so. And whatever the explanation may be, it must always allow for the possibility of a unified self or of a self going to pieces. The disintegrating factors have been explored and exposed in recent times until we all tremble for ourselves and particularly for our children. No generation has ever been so painfully aware of the injuries which, with the best of intentions, we can inflict upon one another and upon ourselves. The treatment given a child at home or at school, or accorded a student by classmates, or meted to an employee, "conditions" him and may inhibit or maladjust him, and produce a mental and moral wreck. The institutions which care for this human wreckage are more and more congested. Books pour from the presses dealing with problems of mental health; practitioners, scientific and quack, abound in our cities. And unquestionably some progress has been made both in diagnosis and in cure. But the victims are such a host, that one is confident that our generation lacks that which prevents folk from going to pieces.

There is a sense in which every man stands over against himself. This is apparent in such words as "self-control," "self-respect," "self-surrender." The disintegration commences when self gets out of hand, and we cannot concentrate our minds on our work, or go to sleep when we should, or bring ourselves to do what we know to be our duty. We may become conceited—a familiar form of disintegration graphically portrayed in the vernacular expression "stuck on one's self." Or we may be awkwardly self-conscious—some of our feelings feeling how the rest of our feelings feel. Or we may seem out of step with our world, like Dickens' Mrs. Gummidge, "the lone, lorn creature," with "everything going contrairy with her and she going contrairy with everybody." Or we may become the thralls of passions which carry us to such lengths that we disown responsibility, and cannot account for what we say or do, and can only confess in language that goes back to a primitive belief in demons: "I don't know what got into me." And undoubtedly there seem to be alien and unmanageable elements in all of us, which explain how the idea of possession arose. We may substitute for evil spirits other words, such as "complex," "phantasy," "fixation," and the like; but the result is akin to that of demoniacs of old—abnormality in the eyes of others and powerlessness to adjust one's self to one's obligations.

On the other hand complete adjustment to environment is undesirable. The creative men and women have always been ill at ease in their world. If society were ideally organized, the individual should try to fit into it; but in things as they are, we ought to be misfits. Here lies the danger in much of the mental therapeutic of our time. It attempts to adjust its patients to the world as it is—to make them normal members of their communities, efficient in their business and contented with their environment. From the Christian standpoint that is to render them worldlings, conformed to an unjust and ungodly and doomed age. Such optimistic extraverts have never been the creators of great art or music or literature, or leaders in social advance.

Religion has a quite different conception of mental health. It adjusts men to God and to the realm of his will. It gives them a sense of strangeness in this world. They are not moved by its incentives. They have their eyes on horizons beyond its skylines. When they look inward they are disgusted with and distrust themselves. Every healthily adjusted life needs, as has been said, both security and stimulus; and these religion offers more effectively than can any mundane social order, however ideal. To believers God is their dwelling place and underneath are his everlasting arms, and stretching before them is the prospect of new heavens and a new earth wherein dwelleth righteousness, which they with God are to create. This is the adjustment to reality which religion offers. There is little question that if children were early made to be at home in God and his eternal purpose, as Jesus reveals them, they would be rendered immune from a multitude of fears, worries, introversions, egotistic dreams, and everyday selfishness which disintegrate character.

And when men are going or have gone to pieces morally, the Gospel is not in the least discouraged. It believes that the worst can be born again new creatures, and that the weakest can find help in every time of need.

It can summon witness after witness whose testimony to its power cannot be gainsaid.

After William James had published his *Varieties of Religious Experience*, Professor Leuba in a review dismissed most of the cases James had cited as mere pathology. James, in a letter to him which modestly understates his own faith, as other letters evidence, wrote:

> "I have no living sense of commerce with a God. I envy those who have, for I know the addition of such a sense would help me immensely. The *Divine*, for my active life, is limited to abstract concepts which, as ideals, interest and determine me, but do so faintly in comparison with what a feeling of God might effect, if I had one." [17]

And the same year he defined what he meant by God as "a combination of Ideality and efficacity," and spoke of God as "a more powerful Ally of my own ideals." [18] His reading of the lives of believing folk had so strengthened his faith in God's living presence that he was unable "to pooh-pooh it away" and found in himself "a germ of something similar that makes response."

"A combination of Ideality and efficacity"—a God who fills our horizon with his perfectness and then is our potent Ally in achieving it for ourselves and for mankind—that is a singularly penetrating interpretation of the Father of our Lord Jesus Christ.

And it is religion as an access of power that our generation most needs. We seem afflicted with pernicious spiritual anæmia. We see any number of stupidities and wrongs in our social order—in international and interracial relations, in the conduct of industry, in the distribution of wealth, in the planning (or rather in the planlessness) of our cities, in the treatment of wrongdoers. The list of recognized social blunders is a long one. Complete solutions may not yet be in sight, but steps which would measurably improve present conditions are plain as day. And yet we halt and hesitate. We seem to have lost our nerve, or to lack initiative, or to be tied up in our own prejudices. What we need is a renewal and release of spiritual energy. Bernard Shaw, in *Back to Methuselah,* lays down the dictum: "Civilization needs a religion as a matter of life and death."

In his fascinating biography of the Adams family, Mr. James Truslow Adams discovers in the third generation, when he is dealing with Charles Francis Adams, our minister to Great Britain during the Civil War, something missing which had constituted the driving power of his forebears. John Quincy Adams, while he saw on the horizon the black clouds of sectional strife, "did not for an instant lose his faith in God and the fundamental morality of the universe." In his son, the war-time minister, the Puritan conscience remained, but the Puritan faith in God was absent.[19] His sons, in turn, were reared without religious belief, and Henry Adams has left us his brilliant but pitiful record of a lifelong search for some clew to human existence. His career, despite great natural gifts and personal charm, lacked altogether the driving force of his ancestors.

Of what use is religion? It is not a utility but a satisfaction—the satisfaction of the supreme fellowship. Those who appraise it as a means to something else, even to such praiseworthy ends as growth in character or as reënforcement for the building of a juster society, hardly know what religion is. The truly devout seek God himself for his own sake. "*Nihil nisi Te, Domine,*" is their dominant request. "My soul thirsteth for God, for the living God." "Man's chief end is to glorify God and enjoy him forever." The distinctive act of faith is adoration—the worshipful intercourse of spirit with Spirit. Such communion is utterly disinterested. Worship demands nothing, claims nothing, and is completely satisfied in God. Like the seraphim in Isaiah's vision, we with awe delight in One high and lifted up and have no occupation but to fly upon his missions. There is no thought of his being useful to us; we are absorbed in being useful to him. God and his glory, in his works and in his ways, about all in his Self-manifestation in Christ, so fill the horizon that we have neither wish for ourselves nor desire for our world that we dare suggest. All and more than we can think is there before us in him and his eternal purpose. Abased and marveling we offer our homage: "Therefore with angels and archangels and all the company of heaven, we laud and magnify Thy glorious Name, evermore praising Thee, and saying, Holy, holy, holy."

This is true religion: fellowship with the living God in the beloved community of his children and in the hallowed company of his creatures—brother sun, sister moon, mother earth, brother wind, air and cloud, calm and all weather, "our sister the death of the body, from which no man escapeth." In the light of the "most high, almighty, good Lord God," as Saint Francis hails him, and of the everlasting righteous society of those who belong to him, we see a meaning in our fleeting years in this world which passeth away, and are empowered to overcome and redeem it, and to live in it as partakers in eternal life.

III

CAN WE KNOW GOD?

WE HAVE BEEN SPEAKING OF THE WORTH OF religion. Many persons to-day acknowledge its value to those to whom it is credible. They often do so condescendingly, much as a physician admits that a housewife's medicinal herb may possess some slight efficacy to relieve an ache. But for themselves they question the truth of religion. They frequently remark that one man's guess about the Unseen is as good as another's. They ask impatiently: Does any man *know* God?

If by knowing is meant "to understand completely," the answer must be a decided negative. None can "find out the Almighty to perfection." But, for that matter, none of us entirely knows his next door neighbor or his own child. All human intercourse consists of voyages of discovery. This is its fascination. Much more is the life with God a series of surprises. The confessions of the devout are full of exclamations of astonishment at One who doeth wondrous things. An apostle, confident that he knew God, found part of his religious satisfaction in that in God which transcended his knowing—his unsearchable judgments and his ways past tracing out. Emily Dickinson wrote in a letter:

> "It is true that the unknown is the largest need of the intellect, though for it no one thinks to thank God." [1]

In the not-yet-known lies the promise of growth in fellowship. Walt Whitman exulted:

> This day before dawn I ascended a hill and look'd at the crowded heaven,
> And I said to my spirit, *When we become the enfolders of those orbs, and the pleasure and knowledge of everything in them, shall we be fill'd and satisfied then?*
> And my spirit said, *No, we but level that lift to pass and continue beyond.*[2]

But can we speak of *knowing* God?

There are various ways of knowing. One is the way of received information—knowledge acquired from those who possess it. A second is the way of exploration—experimenting and discovering for ourselves what is true. A third is the way of insight. We meet a man, or read a poem, or encounter an experience, and we divine the man's character, or the poem's appeal, or the value of the experience for us. A fourth is the way of inference. After we have explored facts, we analyze and classify them and draw a conclusion.

Much has been said of the necessity of our taking the right one of these paths, if we are to reach knowledge of God. As a matter of fact religious people use all four. Nor are they separate paths, but parts of the one road. We begin with religious information conveyed to us out of the spiritual heritage of the race. It was knowledge of this sort of which Professor James was speaking when he said that the whole line of testimony to God's presence was so impressive that he could not "pooh-pooh it away."[3] If we are moved by what is told us concerning God, we begin to try to live with him for ourselves, and make our discoveries of his worth. Most men have hours of insight, when that which they had known by tradition suddenly assumes new significance: they remark, "I never knew before what this meant." Or a truth breaks upon them so startlingly that it seems altogether new. Such was Paul's vision on the Damascus Road. But had he not known of Jesus before, from rumors in Jerusalem and from the Christians he had been persecuting, he would not have identified the light and inward voice with Him.

Again we have critical moods, when we look with detachment at our religious knowledge, and viewing all the data attempt to form a reasoned conclusion. It is knowledge derived in this objective way on which Professor Wieman lays his emphasis. The cosmos impresses him with its unity and the life of men discloses a principle working towards human solidarity, and he feels compelled to acknowledge the "integrating behavior"[4] of the universe. This trend towards the maximum collective good, of which he is certain, he calls "God." Less philosophically minded folk derive similar impressions from the beauty and order of the physical world, from human history and their own experiences of life, and arrive at God as the most reasonable interpretation of their impressions.

It is impoverishing when any of these paths to religious knowledge is barred. We employ all of them in arriving at knowledge in other realms. A scientist is familiar with the information gained from his predecessors: no investigator starts "from scratch." He does his own experimenting and corroborates or corrects his information. He has a flash of insight, which reveals a new principle, or a new application of a principle already known. This he must test and verify. He reasons from all his data and infers his conclusions. A thoughtful believer does the like in acquiring his knowledge of God.

There are, however, differences in the qualifications requisite for knowledge in various realms. The capacities which fit one man to be a laboratory investigator are not identical with those which equip another to be a practising physician. The first is usually more interested in facts than in persons, the latter in persons than in facts. In some realms an impersonal approach, in which the investigator detaches himself as completely as possible from the object of his study, yields most results. In other realms the personal approach is the only one which opens up knowledge. Our sympathy supplies a chief means of understanding.

If one is studying a plant botanically, one's like or dislike of it should be of no consequence. In botany one may hope for a unanimous opinion from all competent investigators. But if one is appraising the plant with a view to cultivating it in gardens, then one's appreciation of it is decisive. There will be no such unanimity among cultivators as to a plant's worth as there is among botanists as to the species to which it belongs. This personal element in appreciation is unpredictable and inexplicable: "There is no accounting for tastes."

The more soaked in personality anything is, the more this taste for it is necessary in order to know it and interpret it. The unmusical cannot understand a symphony; the unpoetical cannot apprehend a sonnet; the unsmitten can form no adequate judgment of a lover. A symphony, a poem, a man's devotion to a woman, are embodiments of personality. Musicians feel an insuperable barrier walling them in when they render a composition to those without an ear. Religious leaders are equally hopeless when seeking to convey their messages to the spiritually unperceptive. Jesus often concluded his parables with the word: "He that hath ears, let him hear." His teaching was the distillation of his own experience, and the essence of his Gospel was a personal fellowship between God and his children. That was possible only for those akin in spirit to their heavenly Father.

Impersonal relations between men inevitably breed misunderstandings and prevent mutual knowledge. The financial or technical expert, competent with figures or machinery, may blunder and cause trouble in an industry by failing to consider the habits and feelings of those engaged in it. Impersonal treatment is a frequent cause of domestic tragedy. A physician and his wife were in martial unhappiness. Both were high-minded, with Christian faith and conscience. Their minister to whom they applied for counsel was baffled. To the query, "What is the matter?" the wife complained, "My husband is forever analyzing me;" and the husband retorted, "My wife is always comparing me with other men." There were the two processes most prized in the scientific approach to knowledge—analysis and classification—and the result was domestic misunderstanding. Love cannot take this detached and impersonal attitude toward its beloved. It says with Edward Rowland Sill:

> So why I love thee well I cannot tell:
> Only it is that when thou speakst to me
> 'Tis *thy* voice speaks, and when thy face I see
> It is *thy* face I see; and it befell
> Thou wert, and I was, and I love thee well.[5]

At the heart of vital religion is a similar personal

devotion. The believer may be undergoing an excruciating ordeal; he may be puzzled to account for moral confusion about him and for prostrating blows which fall on him and his. But a loyal attachment to God holds him fast. An ancient poet in such circumstances prays:

Whom have I in heaven but Thee?
And there is none upon earth that I desire besides Thee.
My flesh and my heart faileth;
But God is the strength of my heart and my portion forever.

Jesus in the darkness at Golgotha, feeling himself God-forsaken, still uses the words of personal trust: "My God, my God."

But this is not to limit our path to religious knowledge to the personal approach. There is need of at least binocular vision to see another truly. We have to use both appraisal and appreciation. The friend who knows us best is not the uncritical admirer, but he who, with affection, looks at us against the background of our place in the world, assesses our work, faces our weaknesses and our abilities, and guides us with counsel that is loving and wise.

Falling in love after the romantic pattern is not of itself an adequate basis for getting married. Two lovers will employ their judgment, and consider whether they can be lifelong comrades, aiding each other to give their utmost to the commonweal. And in marriage an invariably adoring wife, however delightful to the huge masculine appetite for flattery, is by no means the helpmeet who most assists her husband. The understanding wife is at the same time her husband's exacting and frank critic and his constant encouragement and comforter.

In religion it is dangerous to let the discriminating faculty go to sleep. Faith is continually becoming mixed with and debased by superstition, or it is hampered in expression by outworn forms. Hence periods of doubt, when the assumptions of the devout are challenged, often prepare the way for periods of more enlightened and fruitful piety. In them the ground is plowed up and harrowed, and made ready for new harvests. Such periods occur in the careers of most believers, usually during school and college days, and they may recur in later life. When objectors force us to rethink our beliefs and to try to state them more accurately, or when baffling experiences make us question them, while for a time we may be plunged in darkness, we emerge into a clearer and ampler day. Such seasons of mental conflict are common in the biographies of religious leaders. In desperate struggle they win through to a more intelligent and contagious faith. We ought not to grieve unduly over the widespread skepticism of our time. Temporarily it is paralyzing; and paralysis is no light matter when so vastly much waits to be enterprised; but it will bequeath to our successors more true, more assured, and more quickening convictions.

Several suggestions keep recurring to the minds of our contemporaries to confuse them and to interfere with their fellowship with God.

One is that religion is "wishful thinking." We are told that man is born dependent, that he finds it hard to grow up and face the decisions and carry the responsibilities which his parents and teachers carried for him. Life is perplexing, difficult, lonely. When those on whom he has leaned are no longer at hand, he solaces himself by picturing a Being above him, endowed with the affection of father and mother, and he lives in a dream world with this heavenly friend. The phantasy is not deliberately created, but is caught from the group mind which still carries over many crude hopes and fears from the childhood of the race. Religion is a cushion between man and disagreeable reality; it is an escape into which he flees assigning to Providence decisions and obligations he should himself assume.

Many would reply that to them God came as the unwished-for. Conscience faced them with decisions which they did not want to make; they did their utmost to forget them; but there were "strong feet that followed, followed after." Sooner or later they were forced to a Yes or No. And if they said No, the matter was not ended; the Hound of heaven pursued. And the most obedient find God pressing on them that which they would do anything to elude. They are brought to Gethsemanes where the cry is wrung from them: "Not as I will, but as Thou wilt." A God who haunts us as love, coercing us to a more sensitive conscientiousness, to concern ourselves with social situations we would gladly let alone, to embark on courses which expose us to criticism and ridicule and compel us to endless thought and toil, is hardly the creation of our wishes.

But religion may be wishful thinking and be none the less fellowship with a real God. Souls parched by the aridity of life have thirsted for him, and discovered a divinely refreshing Friend. Our attempt to know the mind of any man is wishful thinking. Unless we are drawn to him and interested in him, we do not trouble to try to understand him. All knowledge begins with curiosity—the thirst to know. "Wishfulness," which sounds much worse than its usual form "wistfulness," leads us astray only when we fail to test our ideas by the two criteria to which all conceptions of truth must be subjected; the practical test—Does it work? and the logical test—Is it consistent with the rest of knowledge? A follower of Jesus welcomes these tests. The Gospel insists on results: "By their fruits ye shall know them." It presents Christ as the truth, to be examined in the light of our knowledge. He, the Light of life, illumines for us experiences which, apart from him, are hid in darkness.

A similar disturbing suggestion is that our idea of God is a projection of ourselves upon the heavens. That sounds alarming. Not a few frightened folk go about murmuring that God is man's shadow cast upon the skies. But we come to know our fellow-men by projecting ourselves upon them. We understand another by throwing our feelings, our thoughts, our experiences, toward him and interpreting him through them. Much misunderstanding arises from the failure to project ourselves on those with whom we have to do. We neglect to put ourselves in their place. We treat them impersonally as cogs in the industrial machine, or as conveniences, or as curious specimens of humanity, instead of as fellow-men. We know one another by a process of mutual self-projection. Our usual word for it is sympathy. By sending out a friendly self to them we open the way for them to return it with an answering understanding.

In our efforts to know the rudimentary minds of birds and animals, we project ourselves on them also. Keats tells us:

> "If a sparrow come before my window, I take part in its existence, and pick about the gravel." [6]

There is a grave danger of becoming sentimental and reading our thoughts and feelings into animals. In fact we discover that creatures have an instinctive life which eludes us, and that the most companionable of them—a dog, for example—can return only a fractional comradeship. We find in them meagre beginnings of our personalities.

In religion we project ourselves upon the cosmos in response to that which claims our gratitude and loyalty, in the hope of having fellowship. The most intimately devout discover an "otherness" in God. His thoughts are not our thoughts, nor are his ways our ways. There remains an unbridgeable distance. In part it is the moral chasm between a holy God and sinful men; in part it is the difference between the Infinite and finite creatures. But they are also aware of kinship with God, and they live with him convinced of a mutual understanding. This is not the private secret of an occasional abnormal person, whom we can dismiss as unbalanced. It is the shared experience of a vast company in many lands generation after generation. As they fling themselves upon the Invisible, there is a response. Or rather, as they answer the approach which claims them, they discover fellowship. They report that God remains beyond them, so that they are always reaching up to him, but that he also stoops to meet them. The finer and larger the self which they project toward this mysterious Approach, the more assured and the richer the fellowship. Jesus of Nazareth projects himself and abides with One whom we call his God and Father. In this matter of projection, with what measure we mete, it is measured to us again, and more is given.

Or the same disturbing suggestion occurs in the form that God is only a notion in our own heads. Man through the centuries has evolved a conception of the Highest, and worships this Idea of God, but there is no Reality apart from human minds to whom the Idea corresponds.

Again let us recall that we are to one another notions in one another's heads. If you say that you see *me*, as I stand before you, you remind yourself that you *see* a small image, which the rays of light refract upon the *retinae* of your eyes, and which through the nerves and brain you interpret as me. All that you see is my figure; what I, a person, am for you is a notion arrived at by inference in your head. Through these images in eyes and notions in heads life's intercourse goes on: we do business, make friends, fall in love. That we exist for one another as ideas in the mind does not efface our objective existence as living beings. The net result of a man's intercourse with another is his clew to what his acquaintance is. Our notions of one another change with the richness or poverty of our life together. Experience renders our opinion of a friend more accurate, and enables us more truly to get at him and open to him entrance to our mind and heart.

Existence in its totality makes its impact upon us. We respond sometimes with fear, sometimes with reverence and trust and love. We try to interpret the impact in an image, and project what is at hand in the contemporary situation—the image of a monarch, a shepherd, a builder, a father—perhaps, in a machine age, a process. With growing experience the race changes its images. There has been a struggle for existence among conceptions of Deity and a survival of that image which has seemed best to fit the Being, with which or with whom man has felt himself in touch. What has come through his mental image is man's clew to the mysterious Companion of his fleeting generations. No one image, not even that of father, exhausts all that devout men discover. Christians have received so vastly much through the memory of a Man, Jesus of Nazareth, that they have instinctively let him be to them the image of the invisible God. Throughout the Christian centuries those who have seen God in the face of Jesus Christ, and have worshiped and trusted the Divine thus symbolized, have found him aptly expressing what God proves himself to be. They are mastered by a conviction that God is Christlike. Dealing directly with God in Jesus, and letting God deal with them through him, they have found this image opening to them most enriching life.

Some will say that this is to make God in man's likeness. It is truer to say that this is to seek a symbol to fit what God makes himself mean to us. In every attempt to describe anything we are driven to symbols.

Physicists, trying to picture what matter is like, draw at present their metaphors from electricity; and tell us that masses, to us solid, are open structures with empty spaces and scattered electric charges. In picturing the mysterious effect one person has upon another, we employ such metaphors as "magnetism," "spell," "influence" (a word derived from astrology when subtle potencies for good or ill were supposed to flow down upon human careers from the stars). Religious folk must resort to symbols for the Deity—the supreme spiritual force they know. In human relations the mightiest effects are produced by love. That word seems least inexactly to portray what the Invisible does for and is to us. The loftiest instance of love we know, and that through which the most hallowing effects come to pass century after century, is the career, and especially the vicariously borne cross, of Jesus Christ. Instinctively his followers have worshiped the Most High through him. They have said, "God so loved"; and intrusted themselves to the love of God which is in Christ Jesus their Lord.

In an age concerned with mechanical contrivances run by the power of streams, or of steam, or of electricity, it is not unnatural that many find it congenial to picture both human beings and the universe in terms of machines driven by force. Current attempts to portray the Divinity in man and in the world use metaphors like "the life-energy," "the cosmic urge," "the upward thrust," "the synthetic activity," "the integrating process." But machines and their fuels do not operate without minds who devise and direct them. They are not merely impersonal: they are embodiments of mind. There is something machine-like in the impressions of human society and of the cosmos upon us; but religious folk go past these superficial impressions, and find themselves in intercourse with God, and are aware of his fellowship. It is this fellowship which has supreme significance for them.

We have been insisting that in religion it is impoverishing to part with our critical faculty. At the moment there are a number of thinkers who, under the spell of the gains made by the impersonal and objective approach to truth in scientific investigation, affirm that religious knowledge must be reached by this route alone. They attempt to assess the total impact made by existence upon them as dispassionately as possible, and to report in language free from emotional warmth the results of their analysis and reasoning. One may question whether in religion, any more than in friendship or in love or in any other interest where the heart is engaged, man can prevent his mind from using all the paths to knowledge which it customarily pursues. These thinkers have been reared in the Christian inheritance and cannot wholly divorce themselves from its tradition. They have intuitions, prompted by life's stress or by some of the myriad wakening events of our rousing time. And one suspects that personal tradition and insight enter into their conclusions as well as objective analysis and inference. But their statements have value as a religious minimum from which they cannot escape. As such they may offer a starting point to doubting intellectuals who are deaf to the richer creeds of the more whole-heartedly devout.

They tell us that they find in the universe a creative life which moves toward wholeness. The world contains the possibility of things true, just, lovely, and honorable—things of highest value to men. These emerge in the course of evolution and must therefore inhere as possibilities in the fabric of the cosmos. The source of emergent life, whence derive not only planets and living creatures, but also ideals and consecrations, is to them "God"—a Deity surely known. With this quickening and unifying Power they can become partners. Whether they shall speak of this life-producer as "It" or "He" they are in doubt. They hesitate to deny to it personality; but personality connotes more than the universe discloses; so they prefer for this Divinity of their reasoned knowledge such words as "cosmic élan," "urge to wholeness," and the like. These thinkers are not agnostics, for they assert confident knowledge of "this Power not ourselves which makes for righteousness" of which Matthew Arnold wrote a half century and more ago. Theirs is a different outlook from that of Bertrand Russell thirty years back, when he spoke of man and his hopes as "the outcome of accidental collocations of atoms," doomed to live his brief days in "the empire of chance," and to face the prospect of the ruin of all his achievements under "the trampling march of unconscious power." [7] The Power may still be spoken of as non-personal, but it is "vitalizing" and "integrating." In these near-Theistic thinkers one may hail would-be allies.

Parenthetically one queries whether they are as dispassionate and objective as they fancy. "Wholeness," "integration," betray the desire of a generation which saw the world fall asunder in war, and which has watched it vainly trying to get itself together in finance and in trade and in new political adjustments. Another generation might as surely have marked a differentiating process in the universe, and instead of "a creative Life" an extinguishing Death eliminating species whose day was done and nations whose moral fibre was in decay. Our interests and experiences always determine that for which we have eyes.

Nor can one help questioning whether our supreme values, unknown to us save as qualities of persons—love, justice, hope, a social conscience—become more explicable as possibilities of an evolving universe in whose trend they happen to emerge, than as the character of the creative Spirit—the living God. Are Possibility and Luck more rationally credible deities? Would they "integrate" a cosmos?

These socially minded thinkers illustrate that in our religious knowledge we are dealing with an Object to be known not by the intellect only, but by the whole self. A competent scientific investigator may conceivably be a bad man—selfish, unjust, cruel. Some extremely clever men who know a great deal are morally rotten. But in religion, as in marriage and friendship and in all the intercourse between persons, what a man *is* determines what he can *know.* Sympathy has insights which never come to the unloving. Kindness opens doors which remain closed to the inconsiderate. Only the devoted understand self-sacrifice. Unless a man has a conscience which feels the burden of disunited and suffering humanity, he will not have vision to detect "the integrating behavior" of the universe. Unless a man be wistful for a commonwealth of righteousness, it is unlikely that he will catch sight of "the everlasting creative life that moves toward wholeness." [8]

It is the extent of our response which limits our knowledge of those things that have most worth for us. If we are moved by a painting and taken to depths and heights beyond our usual plane, we know what the artist was attempting to portray, as no coldly assessing critic, however widely familiar with art, can know it. If we recognize ourselves akin to Hamlet, with the native hue of our resolution often "sicklied o'er with the pale cast of thought," and with despondent moods when we ask whether life be worth living, we know that drama of the soul as no bright and buoyant extravert can know it. Emily Dickinson, to quote from another of her letters, wrote:

> "If I read a book, and it makes my whole body so cold that no fire can ever warm me, I know *that* is poetry. If I feel physically as if the top of my head were taken off, I know that is poetry. These are the only ways I know it. Is there any other way?" [9]

She was letting her whole being go forth to know. If we meet a man and report, "I took to him and he to me," we are on the road to mutual knowledge.

It is not otherwise in religion. St. Augustine held that "no good thing is perfectly known which is not perfectly loved." [10] He who tries to leave his heart at home and travel to God with head alone is seriously handicapped. The devout of all the ages are agreed that to know God one must bear him company and share his life. George Fox put it:

> "Though I read of Christ and God, I know them only by a like Spirit in my own soul."

He was repeating the discovery of a New Testament apostle who taught:

> "Beloved, let us love one another: for love is of God; and every one that loveth is begotten of God, and knoweth God. He that loveth not knoweth not God; for God is love."

In his recollections the painter, Sir William Rothenstein, dicussing his own changing estimates of artists, declares that:

> "Knowledge of works of art can be honestly earned by hard work alone. An artist learns, not through books or the opinions of others, but by hourly struggle with the difficulties of actual drawing and painting. Appreciation runs parallel with experience." [11]

If we correct his "not" by "not only," we may say the same of religious knowledge. It is the man who struggles daily with himself and with the lives about him in family, business, church, and community, seeking by love to render them loving, who knows God.

This explains why God is not real to everybody, and may for intervals seem unreal to those who count themselves believers. They lack "eyes of the heart," or such eyes are asleep. Waves of impinging electrons are falling upon all parts of our bodies, but to our ears only are they sound and to our eyes alone are they light. To Milton's devils in Pandemonium it is darkness which is visible. Would they see the light of love, did it shine on them in Christ crucified? What point of contact could Jesus find with such selfish creatures as Iago, or Goneril and Regan, or with sensual worldlings like Falstaff, Mistress Quickly, and Doll Tearsheet? He is silent before the trifler Herod, and unable to be anything but baffling to the expedient Pilate. He cannot bring his Father, so vividly present to him, within the horizon of eyeless hearts.

We may seem to reason in a circle. To become convinced of the Christian God one must already be a Christian. But we are shut up in similar circles in all the spheres where life's best things are known. It is musicalness in himself which enables a man to understand music, and friendliness in himself which recognizes and draws out a friend. Madame de Staël wrote: "Next to genius what is most like it is the power to know and admire it." Next to godlikeness, and on the road toward it, is the power to know the Divine when the light of his face shines upon us. On the threshold of his great experience Augustine pictures himself:

> "Thee when first I saw, Thou liftedst me up, that I might see that there was something which I might see; and that as yet I was not the man to see it." [12]

We have been speaking of the effort to know God as though it were a one-sided attempt on man's part. But Christians insist that it is a double search—God's endeavor to reveal himself and ours to discover him. And it is he who takes the initiative in seeking us. He comes to us in the "given"—in the more-than-deserved which life offers us and in the ideals which claim our consciences. He is "long beforehand" with our souls. The motive within us which turns us toward him is of his prompting. Clement of Alexandria, speaking of the prayer of the mature Christian, one intimate with God, describes it as "Providence returning upon itself," "responsive loyal affection on the part of the friend of God." [13] Luther writes:

> "Before thou callest upon God or seekest him; God must have come to thee and found thee." [14]

Pascal prays:

> "I give Thee thanks, my God, for the good impulses which Thou givest me, and for this very one which Thou hast bestowed to render Thee thanks." [15]

Religion is answer rather than quest.

The devout have found God hard to know, and have confessed, "Thou art a God who hidest Thyself"; but they conclude that the obscurity is in them, not in him.

> Not "Revelation" 'tis that waits
> But our unfurnished eyes.

And these eyes are nothing less than a man's whole self straining Godward. A prophet put it graphically in the phrase, "To stir up one's self to lay hold on the Lord." [16] It is on the single eye that light breaks; it is the pure in heart who see God.

In the second century, when the storm of persecution broke over the little churches at Lyons and Vienne in southern Gaul, their chief pastor, an infirm old man over ninety, was haled before the magistrate's tribunal, where a mob shouted for his death. Asked by the judge, "Who is the god of the Christians?" Pothinus replied: "If thou art worthy, thou shalt know." It was a discerning answer. This old man and his fellow-believers were to endure imprisonment, scourging, the horns of wild bulls, the teeth and claws of lions, roasting at the stake. If the magistrate did not recognize something spiritual in their courage and constancy, and detect divinity in him for whose sake they were prepared to suffer and die, he would not glimpse Deity anywhere. "If thou art worthy, thou shalt know." [17]

And knowledge of God which breaks on man when his whole self responds to the Self-revealing Spirit has to be maintained by fidelity to these insights. No man can once for all become sure of God. If we obey our heavenly visions, they continue master lights of all our seeing. If we neglect them, they turn into the light of common day. It is these

> Fallings from us, vanishings,
> Blank misgivings of the creature,

which puzzle us and cause the seeming unreality of the spiritual world. They may be due to various causes, some within and some beyond our control, but no man who does not live earnestly by the utmost he knows of God remains convinced of him.

One of Yale's foremost teachers of a generation ago began his career with a glowing religious faith and entered the ministry. When called from a pastorate to a chair of economics and social science, he considered himself a Christian believer. But as the years went by and he ceased to take any active part in religious efforts, he found himself slipping into less devout modes of thought and finally without religious interest. In explaining the change which had come over him he said:

> "I never consciously gave up a religious belief. It was as if I had put my beliefs into a drawer, and when I opened it, there was nothing there at all." [18]

There are many who for a time—during student days while they examine critically all their assumptions, or when absorbed in concerns with which Christian faith is dissociated—place their beliefs aside. They do not intend to abandon them; but there is no process by which assurance of God can be kept in storage. Unused faith vanishes.

But even with the earnestly faithful there are apt to be periods of eclipse when the face of God is hid from them. The darkening may be due to the coming of more light; as in physics we learn that under certain conditions light added to light produces not more brightness but darkness, because the rays interfere with each other. Devout people have often been plunged in shadows while they were emerging into an ampler day. They have had to depend on yesterday's sense of God's fellowship in the hope that it would come back to-morrow. God was a memory and a wistful expectation. They had to work and wait by a remembered light.

That, after all, is faithfulness. And the company of the faithful assure us that to the loyal light arises in darkness: the assurance of God returns.

This reminds us that in our knowledge of God, as in other high attainments, the company of the believing plays an important role. Not only do we start with the Self-disclosures which God has made to our predecessors, but we are never sure of our own insights until fellow-seers corroborate them. An artist or man of letters may think as he completes a work that he has caught and interpreted life movingly; but he cannot be sure until others acclaim it. When Fields, the publisher, called on Hawthorne and asked whether he had anything on the stocks, Hawthorne handed him the manuscript of *The Scarlet Letter*, saying:

> "Take what I have written, and tell me after you get home and have time to read it, whether it is good for anything. It is either very good or very bad—I don't know which." [19]

Our religious insights may seem to us luminous, but only as we share them and find other devout folk seeing with us do they become confident convictions. We may feel certain that God is in communion with us, that we hear his voice and are compassed by his love. Then our assurance may fail; such is the ebb and flow of faith; and we may fancy ourselves deluded. But if we discover that our experience is the common possession of many, that it has been the satisfying portion of the faithful for centuries, and is the strength and joy of a world-wide fellowship to-day, we are steadied and confirmed. It is much in religion to say: "I know whom I have believed." It is vastly more to say, "We know," and "to apprehend with all saints" the love that passeth knowledge.

We have been speaking of *our* knowing God; the New Testament is equally concerned with his knowing us. St. Paul writes, "Now that ye have come to know God," and corrects himself, "or rather to be known of God." That surprises us, for we had supposed that all believing men assumed that God knew them.

> O Lord, Thou hast searched me and known me.
> Thou knowest my downsitting and mine uprising,
> Thou understandest my thought afar off.
> Thou searchest out my path and my lying down,
> And art acquainted with all my ways.
> For there is not a word in my tongue, but lo,
> O Lord, Thou knowest it altogether.

But there is a difference between a detective's knowledge of a man he shadows, whose private affairs he investigates and whose mental workings he fathoms, and a friend's knowledge. There is a difference between knowing about someone and knowing him. This Psalm describes God's penetrating knowledge of an unresponsive man. God may know everything about us, and may have love's intuitive understanding of the unloving, but he does not fully know us until we are sympathetic with him.

In one of Mrs. Humphrey Ward's novels, a woman says petulantly to her companion:

> "I thought, Elizabeth, you would have tried to understand me."
> Elizabeth shook her head: "There's only your Maker could do that, Lucy, and he must be pretty puzzled to account for you sometimes." [20]

Are there occasions when we puzzle even God? One recalls the bewilderment of Jesus, who knew what was in man, with his disciples: "Why are ye fearful?" "Why reason ye in your hearts?" "Do ye not yet understand?" "Have I been so long time with you, and dost thou not know me, Philip?" Can his God and Father know those with whom he cannot sympathize? He can appraise selfishness, conceit, snobbery. He knows these from his thousands of years of experience with men from the dawn of human existence on this planet; but he does not know them by appreciation. The devout have felt that the folly of mankind in pursuing roads which lead patently to disaster must perplex their Creator: "Why will ye die, O house of Israel?"

We do not often think of letting ourselves become known to God. But fellowship with him is a mutual affair. We know him by something in us which responds to and interprets him; he knows us by something in him to which we appeal and are intelligible. Jesus insisted upon this mutuality of knowledge: "No one knoweth the Son save the Father: neither doth any know the Father save the Son, and he to whomsoever the Son willeth to reveal him." It is a searching question when we ask ourselves: How well can God know us? What basis in congenial thought and life do we offer by which he can find fellowship with us? Have we a common purpose?

And even in this mutual knowledge, the initiative remains with God. In the saying just quoted, Jesus places the Father's knowledge of him before his knowledge of the Father. God's insight into our aspirations, and his appreciation of our efforts toward truth and love, precede and far outdistance our knowledge of him. We are crude and immature children. Life has to educate us—by responsibilities, by disappointments, sometimes by tragedies, and always by our human contacts—life has to educate us to love, the love that beareth, believeth, hopeth, endureth all, and never faileth. It was after he had dwelt on this love that St. Paul spoke of knowing. And when he did it was to look forward to knowing even as also he had been known. God's knowledge had come first; he aspired to know as he was known.

We mortals are so insignificant amid the swarming myriads of our kind and the vastness of stellar worlds that it remains a wonder of wonders that the mysterious Spirit of the universe should wish personal friendship with us. To suppose it seems outrageous presumption

—egotism exaggerated to megalomania. But the religious of all the ages have been sure of it. It was a central conviction with Jesus of Nazareth. They have known themselves friends of God; and it was he who had sought their friendship, and did everything to keep it. They took a proffered hand; they answered a voice which called them by name; they let themselves be known to One who made advances toward them. They tried to return his amazing friendliness. Martin Luther phrased it: "God knows me right well, and I know him not ill."

IV

IS JESUS AUTHORITATIVE?

A BURNING QUESTION OF THE DAY IS THE place of Jesus in the Christian religion, as that religion is professed by our contemporaries. There can be no question of the place which has been assigned him in historic Christianity. The evangelists tell us that the chief impression made by him on those who listened to him was that of the personal authority with which he spoke. He startled synagogue congregations, accustomed to scribes who quoted the sacred text or the comments of its commentators by prefacing his assertions with "Verily I say unto you." His was the voice of the authentic prophet, indeed of more than a prophet —the unique representative of God. In the New Testament Church, and steadily since, the title associated with his name has been "Lord." In the creeds and hymns and prayers he has been hailed the one Lord Jesus Christ.

But from a half dozen quarters that designation is

declared no longer possible. Historical criticism of the Gospels rightly refuses to accept every saying ascribed to him as a verbatim report. The Gospels have to be assessed as sources for our knowledge of him, and the figure of the Man of Nazareth must be reconstructed and placed in the setting of his time. Many assert that we know far too little of the historic Jesus to take him as an authority. But, admitting the results of this investigation of our documents, it remains true that the figure of Jesus in the entire New Testament has a distinctive religious and ethical quality all his own. It is the same Jesus in character whom we see against the background of heaven in the early preaching of the exalted Lord in the Book of Acts, in the pictures in Matthew and Luke of the Teacher in Galilee, in Mark's graphic description of the tireless Healer of disease and Helper of human need, and in the Creator of new men found in the spiritual experience of Paul and of the Fourth Evangelist. The community of disciples at Jerusalem was disturbed when Paul told Gentile converts that they need not keep the Law, but in his teaching about Jesus apparently Peter and John and James found nothing strange and objectionable. The early Church did not imagine Jesus, but he created the Church, and left his impress on men and women, and through them on this volume of biographies and letters. The Christ of the New Testament is the resultant of the effect of Jesus on those who responded to him. The interpretations of him may vary, but one recognizes the same Jesus in all the documents. The simple reader, equally with the expert scholar, knows what manner of man he was. There is no serious dispute over Christlikeness. There is a faith, a hope, a love which cannot be dissociated from him, and by which men continue to be judged as worthy or unworthy followers of his.

But granting that Jesus can be thus known, it is claimed that with our present outlook upon an immense universe in which our earth is a tiny speck, and upon man's long history with its various crude epochs and successive civilizations, it is ridiculous to ascribe a central position to any single figure in the story of the race, much more to claim for him a central position in the cosmos. Professor Radhakrishnan, an Indian philosopher, lecturing at Oxford, declared that to a modern man to regard either Buddha or Jesus as central in religion is as absurd as to consider our globe central in the universe and man central in the scheme of things.[1] This is no new objection. Among the early assailants of Christianity—Celsus for example—it seemed quite as laughable to fancy that the God of the whole world should become incarnate in a Jewish peasant. But in spiritual matters physical magnitudes are irrelevant and temporal conditions of trifling moment. Personality has more meaning than the sheer bulk of the hugest planet. Little Greece has contributed immeasurably more to human thought than nations many times her size and numbers. That Jesus came of a subject people, inhabiting a small and poor land, is no argument against his spiritual worth for a whole world.

Again it is asserted that in an evolving society no teacher of the past or present can be held a final authority in religion and ethics. This is said to cramp the developing soul and conscience of mankind in an outworn mold. Some sociologists assail the Church as the inveterate foe of progress because it seeks to conform the patterns of individual and social behavior to the "Jesus-stereotype." In other quarters the title "lord" is considered offensive to democratic ears, and classed with the discarded paraphernalia of royalty. Why should a Galilean of the first century "lord" it over our faith and life? A man of letters has written:

> The soul of man is a masterless thing
> That bides not another's control.

Contemporary educators reserve their most scathing attacks for authoritarian teaching. To hark back to this Figure of a remote yesterday, asking what he said and did and was, is to be guilty of "transmissive education," whereas the pupil ought to face his questions freely and make his own creative contribution to the growing knowledge of the race.

Certain missionaries, and especially certain critics of the missionary enterprise, eager to do justice to the noble elements in non-Christian faiths, and humbled by the exalted qualities which they recognize in saints bred yesterday and to-day in these religions, are loathe to press the unique sovereignty of Jesus. In their effort modestly to share with men of other faiths, they tend to set Jesus among a number of religious geniuses, of all of whom we can learn, and to say nothing of his solitary place as King of kings.

In not a few liberal Christian pulpits loyalty to Jesus is seldom mentioned. He is proclaimed as the sublimest figure in history. He is credited with having added more to the spiritual heritage of mankind than any other. Much of his contribution is held to possess abiding value, and to the end of time our race will have cause to be grateful to him. But as a Master to whom we yield final allegiance his day is done. He may be revered as a leader who began a movement and opened a way toward God and man, but he cannot be adored as Lord to whom we give our worship and whose spirit rules our thought and life.[2]

This feeling about Jesus, found only in a few individuals in Christendom in the past, has suddenly become widespread within a single generation. In progressive Christian circles at the end of the last century it was thought that Jesus was just coming into his own as the one Master of men's souls. The Protestant Reformation had substituted the sole authority of the Bible for the authority of the Catholic

Church. Historical study had shown that the Self-revelation of God in the Bible had culminated in the Word made flesh in Jesus. Scholars were insisting that the Old Testament was to be interpreted in the light of the fuller disclosure in him, and Christian people were happily setting aside the cursing psalms and many subchristian passages in the literature of Israel as no part of the message of God to them. There still remained difficulties in asserting the infallibility of Jesus. He apparently ascribed forms of mental illness to demons, and accepted the traditional authorship of the Biblical writings, quoting the Pentateuch as the work of Moses and certain Psalms as by David, while historical scholars denied that Moses or David had written them. But this was satisfactorily settled by saying that, in such matters as the origin of diseases or literary criticism, Jesus shared the opinion of his time. It was only in religion and morals that he was authoritative.

Few had faced what they meant by the word "authority." Whether men spoke of the the authority of the Church, or of the Bible, or of Jesus, it was assumed that religion had to do with mysteries which men cannot investigate and discover for themselves. God had communicated these secrets to special persons—to the inspired writers of the Scriptures, or to the Church through its duly constituted officials. When the infallibility of both Bible and Church was challenged, it was assumed that Jesus possessed information about

God and about man's life with him here and hereafter, which no one else possessed. Hence to call him "Lord" was to take as true what he taught on these subjects, and to obey what he commanded with unquestioning fidelity.

But in the last few decades it has become clear to many Christians that Jesus claimed no authority of this sort. He wished not servants but friends. Could he have them on the basis of submissive obedience? When men attempt out of his occasional and picturesque sayings to construct a theological system or to compile a code to govern society or to regulate their own conduct, they find the sources bafflingly scanty, and they have the utmost difficulty in turning his fluid metaphors into precise laws. If one seeks to draw from his expressed convictions an explanation of the problem of suffering and sin; or if one asks what he taught concerning the ownership of property or the contacts of one race with another, it becomes evident that many of the questions which perplex us were not within his horizon. Can we find in him a clear doctrine of God's relation to the occurrences in what we call "nature"? Can we derive from him a sanction for or a prohibition of the private control of capital, or of the marriage of man and woman who belong to different races? Can we quote him as to the correct method of regulating the liquor traffic, or as to the legislation which should be enacted to govern marriage and divorce in a modern state?

He who looks to Jesus for a set of religious beliefs and a system of ethics is doomed to be disappointed. Jesus is not that sort of authority. Had he set forth a creed which satisfied the minds of dwellers in Palestine in the first century, it would have been out-moded long ere now. Had he announced a code of morals suited to the agricultural and fishing community about the Lake of Gennesaret, it would certainly not fit the industrial society of our machine age.

It is now widely agreed that we cannot formulate either a creed or a code from the teaching and example of Jesus. In Protestant pulpits and Sunday schools it is commonly said that Jesus had certain great religious convictions and consequent ethical principles which he gave to his disciples, leaving them in each age to think out their faith in terms of their time and to apply his principles in the social and personal situations in which they found themselves. And it is wisely added that he promised to conscientious followers his Spirit—the Spirit of truth—to guide them in trying to think and express their beliefs and to discover the Christian way of life for themselves and for society.

It is true that occasionally he made general assertions of his convictions and of his principles. He taught men to call God Father, Lord of heaven and earth, and to live with him in filial trust. He summarized the Law by putting together two Old Testament passages, which bade men love God whole-heartedly and their neighbors as themselves. He uttered the comprehensive Golden Rule: "All things whatsoever ye would that men should do to you, do ye even so to them."

But oftener Jesus' teaching dealt with the situations familiar to his hearers. To encourage persevering prayer he told a story of a man who rapped on a neighbor's door at midnight and by giving him no peace got him out of bed and made him lend him some bread. Such a tale, if not confined to the point Jesus was making, may give a false impression of the gracious and willing Father to whom we pray. This is hardly the expression of a general religious conviction.

A provincial peasant under the Roman Empire might be taken from his work and impressed to transport military baggage. Jesus urged him, if forced to carry so unwelcome a load one mile, to offer to carry it two. In the primitive banking conditions of that time, an agricultural laborer or a small shopkeeper was in the habit of putting his savings into costly garments or into precious ornaments or into a treasure-chest of coins. Jesus warned that moth or rust or thieves might do away with these hoardings, but that there were imperishable spiritual riches. One cannot say that to go a second mile, or "Lay not up for yourselves treasures upon earth," are universal principles. If at times

Jesus laid down principles, leaving his followers to work out their applications, oftener he handled specific cases, leaving his followers to infer from them principles, or rather, to catch from him the spirit in which they might deal with the circumstances which should confront them.

Are we, then, to abandon speaking of Jesus as the supreme authority in religion? Can we, if we try?

To us, as to the men of his time, he speaks with a keen insight which compels attention and assent. Take his delineation of the two characters in the story just mentioned—the householder caught unprovided by an unexpected guest, who in desperation routs out his unobliging neighbor at the dead of night, and this grudging neighbor, also desperate, who concludes that the only way to stop the disturbing banging on his door is to let the persistent fellow have what he wants—they are drawn from life. Jesus holds us by convincing us that he knows what is in man.

He was fond of summing up his observations of life in axiomatic phrases which have become part of the highest wisdom of mankind. For example, he remarked: "Unto every one which hath shall be given, and from him that hath not, even that he hath shall be taken away from him." It is not a romantic interpretation of life, any more than the two characters of which we were speaking were ideal persons. But how true an observation it is!—true of physical health, where plenty of food and exercise build up the robust and prostrate the sickly; true of knowledge, where problems invigorate the trained mind and befuddle the unenlightened; true of character, where temptations develop the conscientious and prove the undoing of the feeble-willed; true of faith, where doubts and difficulties lead the believing on to larger trust and leave the disloyal bewildered, hopeless, cynical. One might multiply instances—for they are as numerous as his sayings—of such acute interpretations of life that persuade us of his understanding. We can no more disregard him than we can brush aside the expert in other realms. He receives from us the spontaneous recognition we accord to one who knows.

At times he disconcerted people by the penetration with which he exposed them. There was that gushing woman who, after listening to him, exclaimed, "How happy your mother must be to have such a son!" and found herself abruptly deflated by the retort: "Yea rather, blessed are they that hear the word of God and keep it." Again and again he shamed men by unmasking them and showing up their emptiness or their selfishness or their idle curiosity. They must frequently have found his company uncomfortable, as we still find it, but he invariably carried their judgment with him, as he carries ours. "That's sound sense," we find ourselves saying—*sound* sense, but not *common* sense. It is his superior insight which grips us. Because he meets us on the current level of our intelligence and conscience, and then takes us vastly further, we cannot help listening to him and letting him open up to us ourselves and our mysterious life.

And when he fully satisfies us as sublimely wise in matters where we already feel capable of checking his knowledge, it is not surprising that we listen respectfully when he speaks of subjects beyond our present experience. Here, too, those who follow him into these less frequented realms do not report him mistaken. Through the centuries there are surprisingly few—one had almost asked, Are there any?—among his sincere followers who have turned back, saying, "We have tried to live under his guidance, and we have found his convictions delusions and his principles unsound." Many have left him because they discovered that his faith demanded more of them than they were prepared to give; but practically none on the ground that his insights were incorrect.

Whatever objections we may have to authority, we impoverish ourselves by turning our backs on those who are masters in their fields—scientific, artistic, practical. In religion not to recognize the authority of Jesus is to doom ourselves to ignorance of the highest open to men in the life with God. As a matter of fact it is always impossible and unthinkable to any who have let him guide them to abandon him as Master of their souls. It is as instinctive for us to own him Lord, whether we employ that word or not, as it was for his disciples in the first century.

Again those whose characters we admire possess a moral superiority which adds weight to their words. The same statement sounds differently from the lips of different men. This cogency has been a quality of the outstanding religious and ethical leaders of the race. What they were made folk listen to what they said, and often made credible what, apart from its illustration in them, would not have been believed. In Plato's *Republic*, Socrates is asserting the essential goodness of God, and one of his hearers, Adeimantus, assents, remarking: "So I myself think, now you say so." [3]

There is a compulsion in sheer goodness which cannot be gainsaid. It commands spontaneous recognition. In the memorable scene in the court room in Victor Hugo's novel, Jean Valjean, who has lived an exemplary life for years and acquired an enviable reputation in the community, confesses himself the perpetrator of the crime of which another is charged, in order to save the accused. And Hugo comments:

> "No one accounted for his feelings, no one said to himself that he saw a great light shining, but all were dazzled in their hearts. Through a sort of electric revelation the whole crowd understood the simple and magnificent story of a man who dies that another may live. All fell back, for there was that divine quality in the incident which causes the multitude to recoil." [4]

This has been preëminently the authority of Jesus.

The sublimity of his character compelled attention and made his words carry conviction. And ever since his sacrifice of himself at Calvary, his teaching cannot be dissociated from the cross. Parables and picturesque sayings, intrinsically beautiful and luminously true, gain a persuasive force because it is he who utters them. Behind them is this life of the Son of man who offered himself. Much that would seem preposterous from another is accepted from him.

Jesus did not hesitate to use this personal authority. "Follow me," was his characteristic invitation to discipleship. He made his own example decisive: "I am in the midst of you as one that serveth." Occasionally he makes assertions which would seem megalomania if they were made by anyone else: "Come unto me, all ye that labor and are heavy laden, and I will give you rest." Such words are convincing because of the Person from whose lips they fall—One who now for centuries has woven himself into the souls of a large section of mankind, and whose tones carry with them the overtones of a vast multitude who avouch his credibility. His authority cannot be separated from what he was, and from what he has been ever since in the experience of thousands.

Further, to Christians he is not a figure of the past only: he is a contemporary alive with power and in fellowship with his people. The memory of the historic Jesus gives content to the risen Lord with whom we are in communion; but in the words uttered centuries ago the Christian hears a present Master speaking to him. C. F. Andrews in his recent autobiography declares:

> "Christ has not been for me simply a great and noble ideal, embodied in an ancient Scripture. He has been to me a living Person, with whom I have held close communion. His voice, when I heard it, had all the authority of his own Passion behind it." [5]

But we must make clear the sense in which Jesus wished to be Lord to his followers, for most of the current objections to assigning him the place of authority in religion are due to misconceptions of the kind of authority which he exercises. It is worth noticing that his characteristic summons to disciples was not "Copy me," but "Follow me." He had to think through for himself the course which he must pursue. The supreme decision of his career, for example—the decision to go to Jerusalem and expose himself to arrest and execution—was not easily reached. In our fragmentary narratives we see him grappling with this problem. His view of the manner of fulfilling his mission runs counter to contemporary expectations. He faces these in the solitary struggle in the wilderness. His closest friends disagree with him and cannot understand him. Up to the last he himself appears uncertain of the outcome. In Gethsemane his mind is canvassing alternatives: "Abba, all things are possible unto thee: take away this cup from me." Step by step he feels his way in fidelity to the God in whom he trusts. As events unfold themselves he decides what his Father wishes of him. His mind flings forth tentative solutions, and he looks at them, waiting for conscience to approve or reject them. He projects possibility after possibility, until his soul rests in one course as linking him with God's purpose, and he prays resolvedly: "Thy will be done."

To follow him is obviously to embark upon a similar daily exploration of events to discover God's will in them. Amid the different circumstances of our age a Christian has to feel out and think through, both for himself and for the various social groups of which he is a member, the course which God would have him pursue. He cannot be an imitator of a Life in the past, but a pioneer in a similarly venturesome comradeship with the living God in to-day. Jesus did not enlist followers to be replicas of himself. The more closely they copied him, the less they would be akin to his innovating spirit. Imitative disciples can never truly represent him. He sought to train men to such maturity of conscience that they would know of themselves what to do and how to do it. So far from stereotyping those whom he influenced to conform to fixed patterns of religious and moral behavior, he did his utmost to develop initiative. And he succeeded. Tertullian well said: "Our Master Christ calls himself Truth, not convention." [6] It was when men saw the *boldness* of Peter and John that they took knowledge of them that they had been with Jesus. The Christians in the Acts and the Epistles are not looking backwards and trying slavishly to reproduce the life of Jesus. They are responding to the promptings of the Spirit of Christ in them. The Christ within them is one in character with the Man of Nazareth, but they do not give an impression of being cramped by an example of a Galilean of a former generation. Freedom is one of their outstanding characteristics. Spontaneously they live as companions of the mind of Christ.

Readers of Walter Pater's *Marius the Epicurean* will recall the occasion when Marius witnesses the gladiatorial games at Rome; and although they are held under the eye of that noble Stoic philosopher, the Emperor Marcus Aurelius, Marius is uncomfortable in their brutality, "weary and indignant, feeling isolated in the great slaughterhouse," angry that Aurelius could be so impassive. And Pater comments:

> "Yes! what was needed was the heart that would make it impossible to witness all this; and the future would be with the forces that could beget a heart like that." [7]

It was this heart which Christianity undertook to create. If we may suppose one of Marius' Christian friends putting a manuscript of the Gospels into the hands of Marcus Aurelius to supply him with rules for the government of the Empire, we can fancy the Emperor's bewilderment and disgust at these collections of conversations and of incidents and accounts of the execution and startling return to His own of a strange Figure. Here is no specific guidance for a statesman; indeed, most of his problems were never envisaged by this Galilean. No! but this Teacher's primary concern is to make over the Emperor, and enlist him with a new spirit to reconstruct the empire.

Jesus is not a giver of laws, but a maker of consciences. He fought external legalism in contemporary Judaism; his greatest interpreter carried on the fight against its reimposition in the Christian Church; and it has been the irony of fate that the Church recurrently tries to make her Lord the sponsor of a new Christian code. His main concern is not to supply new beliefs or new rules, but to produce new men. Hence it is futile to discuss what items in his convictions or his principles were original. Like his own wise householder he was prepared to employ "things new and old." His interest was in a finer conscientiousness—a new quality of life with God and man. By his teaching, by his life, and supremely by his death at Calvary, he himself has become the Conscience of mankind. It is not surprising that the New Testament conceived him as the Judge. Instinctively his followers test right and wrong by him.

This is not to take some saying of his and erect it into a statute for personal conduct, much less to attempt to put it into a legislative enactment for a State. To try to force Christian ideals on men by police powers is contrary to the whole spirit of Jesus. We have to interpret his sayings in the light of what he did, in the light of what he was. Our highest commendation of an act is that it reminds us of him. Our dissatisfaction with any set of human relations—personal, or industrial, or racial—is that they appear unchristlike. Our conceptions of the Most High God are forever being revised in order to make the Father whom we worship as good as his Son. Men dispute over the divinity of Jesus, but all the while it is from him that they gain their loftiest conception of divinity. Jesus has woven himself into our moral judgment. Men cannot get away from him. He sits dominant at the center of our consciences. It is there that he shares the throne of God. Small wonder, then, that he has been pictured at the right hand of the majesty on high! There is no more exalted sovereignty for any Being to whom we bow the knee as God. This is Jesus' authority over us.

And it is important to stress the point that this is not a position to which Christians have consciously elected him. We seem to ourselves to have had little choice about it. It is a position which he wins for himself with each successive generation. We do not so much assign it to him as recognize that he already occupies it. When we confront decisions and make up our minds on religious and moral issues, it is, of course, possible for us to turn our backs upon him and follow our own inclinations. We frequently do. And we attempt to justify ourselves. Why should this first-century Carpenter prescribe our philosophy of life? Why should this "pale Galilean" inhibit our pleasure? But it is not easy to escape him. He haunts us. And we cannot go counter to him without doing violence to our own moral judgment.

He wakes desires you never may forget;
   He shows you stars you never saw before;
   He makes you share with Him forevermore
The burden of the world's divine regret.

Wherever Jesus is known, he is a better than man's best. This gives him his grip on consciences. Despite democratic views which have no place for lords, and despite an independence which brooks no authority, this Man possesses an inherent sovereignty which compels allegiance. To be rebels to him is to wrong ourselves.

If we examine this authority of his more closely, it covers at least three subjects:

First, by discontenting us with anything in ourselves or in society which is at variance with him, he becomes for us the authority on the *goal* of a man's life with God.

To many Jesus is not much more than a nuisance shaming them for acts below their acknowledged standards and troubling them in their godlessness and selfishness. He is a gadfly stinging them out of their complacency. He renders them dissatisfied with their orphan existence in the universe. He provokes them to question current usages and practices. He is worse than a gadfly to those who take him seriously: if in some thoughtful moment they stand face to face with him, they are mortified. They discover and loathe themselves.

They had let God and his will drop out of their calculations. They had acquiesced in the *mores* of their set and community. They had accepted current economic arrangements as the ways in which the world gets its business done; they had slipped into the attitudes taken by folk of one race or class to those of another; they had concurred in the treatment meted out by society to those who transgress its laws and are caught. But in the light of Jesus these matters are on their consciences and plaguing their minds. Men dull their consciences by various self-protecting devices. Convention encases them under a hardened surface. But there is no guarantee that Jesus will not break through this crust and place social conditions and their own lives on their quivering moral fibers.

An elderly Chinese official in the Forbidden City in Peking was once talking with me about spiritual teachers—Lao-tse, Buddha, Confucius. The official was not himself a professed Christian, but he was an intelligent reader of religious books. Speaking of Jesus in comparison with the traditional spiritual guides of China, he remarked: "He seems to me to have the power to create a more delicate conscience." This capacity to render men restive, discontented with themselves and their world, and stinging them to press forward toward a Christlike society, gives him an abiding sovereignty. He is our Master in that he discloses the ideal of fellowship with God and with one another toward which we must advance.

A second subject in which Jesus is an authority is that of the *means* to attain this goal. The route as well as the end must be Christlike.

In the life with God it is not merely that he supplies the image of the God whom we worship and the likeness of the sons of God we are to become, but he also finds us where we are and guides us to discover and live with his Father. As Mrs. Meynell put it:

> Thou art the Way—
> Hadst Thou been nothing but the goal,
> I cannot say
> If Thou hadst ever met my soul.

It is not that he furnishes us with the technique of prayer or charts for us in detail the road each must travel to reach communion with the Most High. His disciples once asked him: "Lord, teach us to pray." What an opportunity to state seven rules for prayer, or to set forth the fivefold method of fellowship with God! Instead he bade them pray with him: "Our Father." They were to discover their own life with God in his fellowship. The path to the Father is a Christlike path—the way of faith and hope and love.

It is not a path of mystic exaltation, but a path of ministry to the needs of men, akin to the Son of man's life and death. Whosoever loveth, with such devotion as we see at Calvary, knoweth God.

In the life with men, too, he is the Way. One can never expect by unchristlike methods to attain a Christlike end. Hence war, however noble the motives which seem to prompt individuals to enlist in it, can never be a Christian method of settling difficulties, nor does it lead to their Christian solution. Class warfare can as little be regarded as a Christian road to an industrial order in which Christian justice and brotherhood prevail. Men do not gather grapes of thorns nor figs of thistles. Anything that intensifies bitterness or fosters strife between classes or races is out of harmony with the mind of Christ. The wrath of man worketh not the righteousness of God.

An honest facing of existing social situations reveals conflicting interests. Many idealists believe that only by stimulating these conflicts can an ultimate peace of justice be procured. But for the Christian, Jesus is authoritative not only for the ideal to be sought, but also for the method of its attainment. Matthew Arnold rightly stressed the "sweet reasonableness" of Jesus. His means as well as his end are friendly. Violent coercion (civil war under another name) is impossible for those who are his followers. We are committed to seek the city of God in paths plainly marked by Christlike love. Here again his guidance is not detailed nor specific. One cannot find in him a political platform or an economic program or a charter of an ideal commonwealth. Progress in all these spheres demands careful use of the tested experience of mankind. Troeltsch phrased it well when he wrote:

> "Nowhere does there exist an absolute Christian ethic, which only awaits discovery; all we can do is to learn to control the world situation in its successive phases just as an earlier Christian ethic did in its own way." [8]

Those who follow Christ's light see the direction in which they must move, and the spirit in which they must advance.

A third subject in which he is the authority is that of the *resources* which are available for this advance. He furnishes his followers with limitless supplies of courage and patience. Indeed he is himself the embodiment of the wisdom and power they need. With him they find God near, and through him God's might is mediated to them.

A distinguished Jewish preacher in Chicago, Dr. Solomon B. Freehof, in his book *Stormers of Heaven*, gives this objective witness to the power Christ affords his disciples:

> "The consciousness of the presence of God has come to millions of men and women through Jesus. . . . He is still the living comrade of countless lives. No Moslem ever sings, 'Mohammed, lover of my soul,' nor does any Jew

say of Moses, the Teacher, 'I need thee every hour.' . . . He brought God near to men through his presence. He made the Divine personal for myriads of worshipers." [9]

This is impressive testimony from a sympathetic outsider to that sense of adequacy through Christ for the quest of the impossible ideal which was voiced centuries ago by an apostle: "I can do all things in him that strengtheneth me."

And One with such mysterious authority as to the goal of life and the path and power to its achievement inevitably raises questions as to who he is. Is he a fortuitous happening in the evolution of our race—one who chanced to come on the stage centuries ago and has chanced to hold this spiritual lordship over thousands in each generation since?

Those who have yielded themselves to his authority have never been content with such a casual explanation. They find themselves offering him an homage beyond which they have nought to proffer. Spontaneously they cede him their utmost reverence and fealty. God Most High can evoke no more from them. And for them Jesus is God manifest in Man—the Conscience not only of mankind, but the Conscience in control of the universe. This is a leap of faith, but it is a leap which the vast majority of Christians throughout the centuries have felt impelled to take. Such faith alone seems to them to do justice to One who reveals the goal of life, the way toward it, and furnishes power to attempt its attainment. In following him they are persuaded that they have embarked on no uncertain quest and are enlisted in no losing cause. They have been open-eyed to the obstacles that barred the progress of their enterprise, agreeing that "If way to the Better there be, it exacts a full look at the Worst." They have never been optimistic about its contemporary victories. From the day when an early disciple wrote, "The whole world lieth in wickedness," down to our own time when we are painfully aware of titanic forces assaulting the Christian ethic and a vast lethargy oppressing its professed devotees, Christianity has seemed threatened by all-but-insuperable powers of darkness. Calvaries dot the course of Christian history, and there is no reason to fancy that the future on this planet will differ in this respect from the past. But the cross has never been the end of a chapter in human affairs. It has been the beginning of a further advance. Through all vicissitudes *vexilla regis prodeunt.*

When we ask why this has been the case, we can only tell ourselves that it is because this strange world of ours is so built. We are compelled to place the figure of Jesus in a cosmic setting. This has been true of all the Christologies from the first century to our own day. This Master of men is Lord of the universe, or his own faith is God in vain.

And it is this cosmic setting of the figure of Jesus, as well as his own inestimable worth to them, which compels Christians to attempt to spread his sway over all peoples. He belongs to the whole world and the whole world belongs to him. This seems arrogant to those who are not his followers. They suggest that we stabilize the *status quo* in religions, letting Buddhists and Mohammedians, Jews and Christians, remain within their ancestral faiths, and seeking sufficient points of agreement to unite them in spiritual fellowship to promote human well-being. And surely no intelligent follower of Jesus can allow himself to be contemptuous of the sincere faith of any man, nor fancy that he cannot learn from him, nor be unwilling to work with him for any end which is dear to the heart of his Master. Nor should we picture Christianity as an aggressive and imperialistic religion, going forth to conquer for its Lord the adherents of other faiths. That is to misrepresent the mind of him who sketched the Good Samaritan. But from the beginning those who have found the lordship of Jesus the source of new life have felt it impossible not to share him with all men. Such sharing has never meant that Jesus could be placed alongside of various spiritual leaders in men's reverent regard. He never will divide a soul's allegiance with others. Wherever Jesus becomes a force in human life, he takes an exclusive supremacy. He does not displace other teachers and guides of the spirit; he comes not to destroy but to fulfill; but they inevitably occupy subordinate positions in the now Christian soul, to whom he becomes

Lord of lords. How can it be otherwise when his disciples discover in him the God they adore, and he is to them the disclosure of the controlling Spirit of the universe?

Nor is Christianity's main conflict to-day with other religions. The issue the world over is between those who share Thomas Hardy's feeling that ours is a "nonchalant universe," and those who believe that in and above all is One who cares. This is not a belief easily held by any who think. Here are pain and wrong and frustration which defy explanation. Here is a cosmos that appears morally indifferent. The central symbol of our faith—the cross—recalls an experience of seeming defeat and desertion. But that cross becomes to those who are mastered by Jesus the most revealing disclosure of the ultimate Reality. Put side by side two such sayings as, "My God, why hast thou forsaken me?"—the feeling of the Sufferer himself—and "God so loved the world"—the impression of those who viewed the event in the light of its consequences. Here they are cogently shamed with themselves and their world, guided to live and labor in the uttermost devotion, and empowered to hope and strive for a society dominated by such love as the cross symbolizes. They cannot demonstrate to others that the universe is not uncaring. They can only bear witness that it has not been so with them, that they have known a love given to them freely, beyond any human affection, and that the supreme inspirations come to them in the figure of Jesus. They grant that their interpretations of him, like all their knowledge, are provisional and open to amendment. Here, as in everything else, they know in part. Nevertheless they *know*. The worth of Jesus is to them beyond question. His place in their hearts is assured. For them he is Lord now, and some day, however distant, they are convinced that he will be Lord of all.

V

WHAT IS SPIRITUALITY?

THIS IS A WORD SO COMMON IN THE VOCABULARY of many devout people that it provokes those who hear it. It is used rather vaguely and with various applications. A school-teacher is said not to be very stimulating to the intellects of his pupils, but to exercise a spiritual influence over them. A church is praised for the many helpful ministries it performs for its community, but its congregation is alleged to lack spirituality. A man is admired for his civic devotion, but the godly regret that he is not spiritually-minded. Is it surprising that we hear the question put somewhat petulantly: "What do you mean by spirituality? What makes a man spiritual?"

Instead of attempting a definition, let us begin by examining some characters in our Christian classic who are spoken of as outstanding instances of spirituality.

If we go back to Israel's primitive tribal days, among the heroes of the clans of that iron age one figure is connected with the Spirit of God oftener than any other. Had we asked a member of the tribe of Dan to point out to us the most spiritual man in the clan, he would have shown us Samson. Perhaps there is no Biblical character whom modern Christians would be less likely to think of as an exemplar of spirituality. Recall this Hebrew Hercules with his prodigious muscular strength, with his coarse and sometimes cruel sense of humor, shown when he caught foxes, tied them in pairs with firebrands fastened to their tails and set them loose in the Philistine grainfields, or when he rose at midnight in Gaza, picked up the gates of the town, bar and all, and carried them to the top of a neighboring hill for the amazed inhabitants to stare at in the morning; with his sensual nature, leading him into amours no more creditable to his loyalty and self-control than those of Homeric warriors; with his fitful patriotism, now espousing the cause of his oppressed fellow-tribesmen and terrifying the Philistines, now lapsing into his own self-indulgent pursuit of women. What a strange figure to be recalled in the annals of a nation dedicated to the God of righteousness, and to be enrolled among the heroes of faith by a writer in the Christian New Testament! And four times in the brief narratives which record his career it is said that the Spirit of God came upon him.

It is usually in connection with some startling feat of physical strength. "The Spirit of the Lord came mightily upon him," and he took hold of a lion in his bare hands "and rent him as he would have rent a kid." "The Spirit of the Lord came mightily upon him, and he went down to Ashkelon and smote thirty men." The Philistines capture him and bind him with ropes, "and the Spirit of the Lord came mightily upon him, and the ropes that were upon his arms became as flax that was burnt with fire. And he found a new jawbone of an ass, and put forth his hand and took it, and smote a thousand men therewith."

According to the thought of the epoch when this story was told, and of the later day when it was compiled in a sacred history, here is a typical instance of spirituality. But would those accounted spiritual in our day recognize a kinsman in Samson! What place could be found for him in so-called spiritual institutions? He would shine under certain circumstances as a counselor at a boys' camp, or as the physical director of a Young Men's Christian Association; but what parents would intrust their young hopeful to his spiritual influence, or what board of management would pass his character? He might be useful as the doorkeeper of a Rescue Mission, where obstreperous persons have to be summarily handled, but the spiritual would feel that none in the audience needed conversion more than he.

It is well to begin our study of spirituality with this crude clansman, far below the Christian level, for the conception was linked with physical robustness and abounding vitality, and these must never be dissociated from it.

A number of centuries later, in Israel's exile in Babylon, her priestly historians are chronicling the beginnings of her ecclesiastical institutions, one of which was the Tent in which hallowed objects were housed before the Temple was built at Jerusalem. One of these writers speaks of the craftsman who designed it, Bezalel, as a man of extraordinary spiritual endowment. He makes Jehovah say to Moses:

> "See, I have called by name Bezalel, the son of Uri, the son of Hur, of the tribe of Judah: and I have filled him with the Spirit of God, in wisdom and in understanding and in knowledge, and in all manner of workmanship, to devise cunning works, to work in gold, and in silver, and in brass, and in cutting of stones for setting, and in carving of wood, to work in all manner of workmanship." [1]

It is not said that Bezalel had anything to do with the offerings or prayers in the Tabernacle; he could not, for he did not belong to the hereditary priesthood. His spirituality was shown in his eye for beauty and in his skill to create it.

Incidentally one cannot help feeling a pathos in the career of the Israelitish artist. It is likely that he had been an apprentice in some *atelier* in Egypt where, as our modern world has reason to know from the glorious treasures unearthed from its tombs in recent years, art had reached a high stage of development. This Hebrew boy's æsthetic nature had been awakened, and he had become proficient as a craftsman in several lines. It must have been harder for him than for most of his fellow-slaves, doomed to dull brick-making, to leave a land of massive temples and pyramids, where the arts were cultivated in painting and sculpture, in jewelry and furniture and in many wares, and face the life of nomad tribesmen. And when at Sinai among the fundamental Divine enactments for the life of the new nation he heard the sweeping prohibition,

> "Thou shalt not make unto thee a graven image, nor any likeness of anything that is in heaven above, or that is in the earth beneath, or that is in the water under the earth,"

his artistic nature must surely have felt cribb'd, cabin'd, and confin'd. Then suddenly there came to him this opportunity to be an interpreter of the beauty of form and of color and of the combination of materials in this Tent of Meeting, as it is pictured in the subsequent tradition. Men recalled, and told their children, age after age, how marvelously he wrought with the scanty resources at hand afar from the marts of the world. His name was handed down as a striking instance of spirituality.

It is an instance which many, especially among Protestants, would not have recognized. They have often disparaged the æsthetic as unrelated to the spiritual. Sir Edmund Gosse, reared in an extremely earnest, although very narrow, ultra-evangelicalism, tells us that at sixteen he found himself torn between a sensuous love of beauty and a devout desire to further Christian faith:

> "In my hot and silly brain Jesus and Pan held sway together, as in a wayside chapel discordantly and impishly consecrated to Pagan and to Christian rites." [2]

But a truer interpretation of spirituality would have made plain to him that there is no such unwholesome antagonism between the lovely and love. Bezalel consecrated his artistic taste and skill to the service of the God who is both righteousness and beauty. We must make room for æsthetic gifts in our conception of spirituality.

For a third example we pass to the New Testament. After the outpouring of the Spirit at Pentecost, the man on the pages of the Book of Acts who is described as "full of the Spirit" is Stephen. The epithet is applied in an interesting connection. Ill-feeling had arisen in the primitive Christian community in Jerusalem over the distribution of a dole: "There arose a murmuring of the Grecian Jews against the Hebrews, because their widows were neglected in the daily ministration." It was a delicate situation where men of tact were needed, with an unquestionable reputation for justice—"men of good report, full of the Spirit, and of wisdom." And among the seven chosen for these qualifications the first is Stephen. Are fairness and discretion often regarded as signs of spirituality?

And Stephen illustrates much more. There is an unconscious humor in the account of him in the Book of Acts. The apostles had said in a superior tone that, since they were preëminent preachers, they ought not to be cumbered with relief work: "It is not fit that we should forsake the word of God, and serve tables." But as one reads on, one discovers that the preacher in Jerusalem whom the crowds flocked to hear was not one of the original twelve, but this supposedly inferior Stephen. And he was a convincing speaker: "They were not able to withstand the wisdom and the Spirit by which he spake." "Wisdom" here is the intelligence shown in his grasp of the meaning of history and his ability to marshal its data with cogent logic to send home his conclusion that Jesus is the Messiah, summing up the hopes of Israel's long expectation. The speech attributed to Stephen is a masterly *résumé* of some two thousand years of religious history, used with persuasive force. The content of the adjective "spiritual" must be widened to include painstaking study and orderly thought—the spirituality of the intellectual.

Nor is this all. When the mob turns upon Stephen and he is being stoned to death, he sees "the glory of God, and Jesus standing on the right hand of God"—a penetrating insight. "And he kneeled down, and cried with a loud voice, Lord, lay not this sin to their charge" —a sublime forgiveness. How comprehensive spirituality must be to embrace the justice and tact, the scholarship and logic, the intuition and charity of Stephen "full of the Spirit."

If we turn a page or two in this narrative in Acts, we find another man, Barnabas, mentioned with the same epithet. And it is given him, too, in a suggestive situation. The original disciples of Jesus had all been Jews, but in Antioch Gentiles were applying for admission to the Christian Church. This puzzled the leaders, who, then as always, hesitated at the unprecedented. When Simon Peter was bid by a heavenly vision go to a Roman centurion, he replied, as religious folk all too often answer: "Not so, Lord; for I have never—" It did not occur to him that it is presumptuous for any man to confine God within his own small tradition. And when at Antioch these outsiders began to come in numbers, the apostles at Jerusalem were at a loss to know what to do: "Must Gentiles first become Jews before they can be Christians?" They remembered that they had at hand a man, brought up on Gentile soil in Cyprus, who had already shown himself apt at welcoming recruits in his treatment of Saul of Tarsus; and they sent Barnabas off to Syria. He was no brilliant thinker to determine a policy on principle. The main question at stake had to wait until a university trained mind—that of the distinguished pupil of Gamaliel—thought it through, and settled the status of non-Jews on a par with Jews in the Church. But Barnabas is a great-hearted soul, whose instinct guides him, even when his intellect cannot arrive at reasons. In these wistful followers of Jesus, "he saw the grace of God, and was glad." A narrower man would not have been pleased to see God graciously working in an unexpected area. He did not know what to say with reference to the necessity of the Jewish law for these new Christians, and wisely he said nothing. But he was confident of one essential: "He exhorted them all, that with purpose of heart they should cleave unto the Lord; for," adds the narrator, "he was a good man, and full of the Holy Spirit." His spirituality is shown in his discernment of God's working along unusual lines and in his hospitable heart.

Samson, Bezalel, Stephen, Barnabas—what diverse types to be labeled with the same adjective—"spiritual." Obviously they are on different planes of religious development: Samson and Bezalel are primitive tribesmen, while the two Christians have been lifted by the life and cross of the Son of God. But what have these four exemplars of spirituality in common?

First, *consecration.* Each of them took his endowment—Samson his strength, Bezalel his art, Stephen his intellect, Barnabas his heart—and dedicated it to the cause of God as he understood it. Their capacities were not in themselves spiritual. Strength, art, intellect, kindliness may be debased to ignoble ends. They became spiritual when devoted to the Divine purpose. Nor is spirituality a characteristic or quality added to our other gifts: it is the new direction given to our whole being. These four men gave themselves to the tasks they considered God's work. Samson attacked the oppressors of his clan; Bezalel provided a beautifully symbolic shrine for the sacred objects of Israel's worship; Stephen by helpfulness, cogent reasoning, and loyalty to death advanced the Church of Christ; Barnabas opened its doors in welcome to would-be followers of Jesus. Dedication of as much as in us is to God's purpose is the first component of spirituality. Browning put it in the lines:

> Religion's all or nothing; it's no mere smile
> Of contentment, sigh of aspiration, sir—
> No quality of the finelier tempered clay
> Like its whiteness or its lightness; rather stuff
> Of the very stuff; life of life, and self of self.

Second, *inspiration*. In all four men those who described their careers were aware of the Divine Presence. Samson, Bezalel, Stephen, Barnabas, were themselves *plus*—*plus* the indwelling and active God. It was not only Samson's huge physique that battled spectacularly for enslaved Israelites, but Samson reënforced. It was not Bezalel's taste and skill alone which adorned that sacred Tent, but Bezalel augmented. In the services of Stephen and Barnabas to the infant Church, their successors saw not just their signal powers, but also the outpoured Spirit. When a man gives himself devotedly to tasks which seem to him God's assignment, the Spirit, which is a Jewish word for God present and operant, works through him. He is "by some nameless difference born anew." Consecration and inspiration are the manward and Godward aspects of spirituality.

On one side we are ourselves *active* in this experience of the Spirit of God. A man has to place himself at God's disposal. We see this not only in these four instances, but in the supreme illustration when Jesus, leaving his private interests in the carpenter's shop at Nazareth, devotes himself with a penitent people at the Jordan to seek a higher righteousness for the nation.

On another side it is an experience in which we are *passive*—or rather in which immeasurably more than we do is done for and through us. We are owned and used by Another. At the Jordan the evangelists recall that the Spirit of God came upon Jesus, and they represent him going away with a sense of vastly increased capacity: "And Jesus returned in the power of the Spirit into Galilee." He stands in the familiar synagogue in Nazareth, and reads of himself the prophet's words: "The Spirit of the Lord is upon me."

This combination of working and seeming to be worked upon and through is not confined to those whom we think of as religious leaders. There are instances of it among scientists. Darwin's son describes his father toiling "as if an outside force were driving him."[3] Von Helmholtz said of himself:

"Happy ideas come unexpectedly without effort like an inspiration, so far as I am concerned. They have never come to me when my mind was fatigued or when I was working at my table." [4]

Similar statements have frequently been made by men of letters. Sir Walter Scott confessed:

"I have repeatedly laid down my future work to scale, divided it into volumes and chapters, and endeavored to construct a story which I meant should evolve itself gradually and strikingly, maintain suspense, and stimulate curiosity; and which finally should terminate in a striking catastrophe. But I think there is a demon who seats himself on the feather of my pen when I begin to write, and leads it astray from the purpose." [5]

And elsewhere he wonders whether his fingers set up for themselves, independent of his head, for, beginning with a certain plan, he never adheres to it for half an hour. Thackeray asks:

"I wonder do other novel-writers experience this fatalism? They *must* go a certain way, in spite of themselves. I have been surprised at the observations made by some of my characters. It seems as if an occult Power was moving the pen. The personage does or says something, and I ask, how the dickens did he come to think of that?" [6]

His contemporary, George Eliot, declared:

"That in all she considered her best writing there was a 'not herself' which took possession of her, and that she felt her own personality to be merely the instrument through which this spirit, as it were, was acting." [7]

In the next generation, Robert Louis Stevenson, speaking of his story, *Kidnapped*, says:

> "The characters took the bit in their teeth; all at once they became detached from the flat paper; and they turned their backs on me and walked off bodily; and from that time my task was stenographic." [8]

One could name a succession of English poets from Milton to Masefield, who, when handling their highest themes, begin with an invocation to the Spirit of God. Nor is this confined to men in the Christian heritage. It is both older and more universal. We are told that a Greek sculptor, on completing a statue, would kneel down before it, recognizing in its beauty not merely the creation of his hands, but also an expression of the Divine. It is a common recognition on the part of the creative spirits of the race. They would accept Emerson's familiar explanation of Michelangelo's work as architect of St. Peter's:

> Himself from God he could not free.
> He builded better than he knew.

There is an extensive body of evidence, drawn from men in many callings, of a *plus*, which implements man's powers when he is giving them unreservedly to a high task. Nor should we be surprised to discover spirituality in realms not immediately identified with religion. In our four Biblical characters we have instances of the major interests of human life—the physical, the æsthetic, the intellectual, the social—becoming spiritual. Life cannot be divided into the secular and the sacred. Religion may be secularized by unspiritual believers, and all life may be spiritualized by those who dedicate it to holy purposes. No doubt there is much unconscious spirituality—the working of the Spirit through devoted men who are unaware of their inspirer. They gain in confidence, in restfulness, in an exalted sense of mission, when they become conscious of Him who works in them.

> Like a vessel at the launch
> When its last restraint is gone.

Giving God their best, they are sure that the result will be better than they know.

In selecting these individual illustrations of spirituality we have risked overlooking its social character. There is no instance of an isolated spiritual individual. The unique endowment of a Jesus is mediated through the nation and church and family. The Spirit is the corporate possession of a group, and the individual's opportunity to become spiritual lies in his membership in the body. "L' Esprit Saint c'est Dieu social," wrote Vinet. Our four characters were all members of spiritual fellowships—a dedicated clan, or nation, or church. We participate corporately in the life of God. There is a double process to be borne in mind: the spiritual man draws his supply of the Spirit from God through the group to whose highest ideals he consecrates himself: in turn he further spiritualizes the group who become more responsive to the Spirit of God through him.

The first and most influential of social groups is the family. Its present form is the result of a long process in which mankind has tried various types of domestic unity, and the monagamous family has shown itself fittest to survive. But even when this is sanctioned by religion, it is not necessarily spiritual. Many families are only biological or economic groups. Man and woman have been drawn together by sexual attraction, and the family is maintained by parental instinct and mutual dependence. Other families are companionships, where man and woman choose to live together so long as they find one another agreeable mates. They may not wish children, or if these come, they feel no obligation to provide them with two permanently united parents. They may even declare it degrading to continue to live together after "love" dies. This exaggerated individualism fails to recognize in the home a spiritual ideal superior to one's self to which is owed a loyalty not to be set aside.

At the opposite extreme are families based on some social reason, where marriage is sought, not for companionship, but because man and woman consider it their duty to community and country to found a home. Robert Burns declared that

To make a happy fireside clime
  For weans and wife—
That's the true pathos and sublime
  Of human life.

One would not deny its high ethical value, but it is not yet the sublime of human life; that arrives with the spiritualization of the home.

The spiritual family is constituted by the lifelong union of man and wife in body, mind, and soul, forming a spiritual organism—the home, dedicated to be the prototype and creator of the spiritual society—the commonwealth of God. It subsumes and completes the partial and inadequate ideals of the family. It is a biological union where sex attraction is recognized and hallowed. It is a companionship of minds for which equality in culture and congeniality of interest are necessary. It is an economic partnership where burdens and resources are shared. It is supremely a comradeship in faith and purpose—each strengthening the other in God and his righteous will for society. Only of man and wife bound thus can it be said, "those whom God hath joined together."

Such a marriage creates a spiritual organism, sometimes called "a joint personality." This becomes the unit of spiritual society. No home can live unto itself. A self-centered family is like a stagnant pool in which the affections lose their lofty purity. The home must be dedicated, and its affections, to be the vehicles of the

Divine Spirit, must consecrate the beloved to the community and nation and the world-wide family of God. Homes, like all social groups, tend to become selfish. Family affection is easily degraded into nepotism. One has only to scan the rolls of public employees to discover the number of relatives of Congressmen, or to observe our large business enterprises, to see the lucrative positions to which kinsmen of the principals are appointed. Parental love rarely sets before sons and daughters sacrificial careers. In high and holy endeavors a man's foes are frequently they of his own household. But, as with the individual, the spirituality of a home consists in its consecration to the service of God in the commonweal, and its consequent indwelling by his Spirit.

Because the family is the unit of spiritual society the individual owes it a devotion prior to any other human obligation. "He that provideth not for his own, and specially they of his own household, hath denied the faith, and is worse than an infidel." Dedication under God of husband or wife, parent or child, to the home brings self-development. The survival value of the permanent spiritual family lies in what it achieves for the characters of its members, and through them for the enrichment of society.

The indissolubility of the home is essential if it is to be a school of character. Its object is not to render life easier, but to make it better. Chesterton has written with arresting exaggeration that "the family is a good institution because it is uncongenial." Inasmuch as it is composed of growing and changing personalities, there must be constant mutual adjustment. William James, in a letter to his daughter, said: "It is good sometimes to face the naked ribs of reality as it reveals itself in homes." Home adjustments are frequently difficult. George Eliot commented of the Bede household:

> "Family life has often a deep sadness in it. Nature, that great tragic dramatist, knits us together by bone and muscle, and divides us by the subtler web of our brains; blends yearning and repulsion; and ties us by our heartstrings to the beings that jar us at every moment." [9]

But the spiritual family holds together. Its permanency rests not on the fusion of romantic passion: this may die; it will certainly ebb and flow:

> There lives within the very flame of love
> A kind of wick or snuff that will abate it.

It recedes into the background with advancing years. Nor is it based on mutual liking. Here are developing persons, never entirely compatible, but maturing their finest qualities in mutual consideration.

The Christian ideal of the family was called by Renan "overstrained morality." It might seem so to the unspiritual. But we have been insisting that in spirituality there is both man's effort and God's inspiration. Ideals are not only goals for our striving, but also gifts of God's grace. There is no overstrain where the requisite resources are freely supplied. The spiritual family cannot be imposed by legislation upon an unspiritual people. It is the achievement of those who dedicate themselves to it in faith that through them God's Spirit works exceeding abundantly above all that they ask or think.

The family is held together by loyal love: its members are loyal to one another under loyalty to God and to his ideal society. Such love abides changes, endures strains, and is ready for redemptive sacrifice. The individual curtails his freedom that he may attain a higher spiritual liberty. Binding ties do not cramp which unbind the holier selves within. Acceptance of such ties does not repress individuality. It would seem hard to surrender one's individuality to another person; but the surrender is made to the spiritual partnership—a very different matter.

The spiritual home is the chief producer of spiritual men. Of the only one of our four Biblical examples of whose parentage and childhood we have any record it is clear that Samson's spirituality is traceable to his dedication by Manoah and his wife, to their nurture of him in the faith of Israel, and to their providing him with a reminder of his religious vocation. With Jesus the home was his sacrament of the Divine Society, from which he drew his words for the highest relationships:

Father, brother, love. It furnished him with the prototypes of spiritual kinship: "Whosoever shall do the will of God, the same is my brother, and sister, and mother." In the spiritual family we gain our richest experience of human fellowship. Thomas Carlyle, recalling his home in Ecclefechan, wrote:

> "Thank heaven, I know and have known what it is to be a son and love a father as spirit can love spirit. God give me to live to my father's honor and his!" [10]

And one of our discerning contemporary ethical teachers, Dr. Felix Alder, finds married life on the spiritual level inevitably opening the door and furnishing the insight to forefancy the perfected society. Of aging man and wife he writes:

> "Together they have traveled the road of life, and remembrance now holds them close, remembrance of many hours of ineffable felicity, of a sense of union as near to bliss as mortal hearts can realize, of high aspirations pursued in common, of sorrows shared—sacramental sorrows. And now, nearing the end, hand in hand they look forth upon the wide universe, and the love which they found in themselves and still find there to the last, becomes to them a pledge of the vaster love that moves *beyond* the stars and the suns." [11]

A second social unit which affects the spiritual status both of the individual and of mankind is the nation. A common habitat and history have unified this larger group and developed a corporate character different from that of every other nation. This national character is both effect and cause of the characteristics of its citizens, and to the extent that its distinctive traits are valuable, the nation's continued existence is justified. The world would be the poorer were it to cease to be. Its character impels the nation to its own experiments in political and social action. Patriotism, the devotion of the individual to the national enterprise, was the spirituality of Samson and of Bezalel. The one set himself to free his fellow-clansmen from oppression that they might pursue their tribal destiny unthwarted by alien tyranny; the other gave himself to the artistic enrichment of his people in their nomad shrine. But both politics and religion have undergone a long development since their day: Christian patriotism employs methods that accord with those of Jesus and it has other and more inclusive horizons.

Nationalism has two inherent necessities which may become perils to spirituality. One is the need for inner unity. If the nation's will is bent on a particular form of social life and course of political action, it is naturally intolerant of those within its borders who are at variance with its mind. The nation's self-respect demands loyalty of its citizens. To be at odds with the national conscience seems criminal. But this condemnation may fall on those who are in advance of, equally with those who lag behind, the corporate purpose. Socrates in Athens and Jesus in Jerusalem are held enemies of the nation. Insistence upon unity proves a nation's undoing when it breeds impatience of variety of opinion and frank criticism of the national life which are essential to its healthy growth. A nation may become afraid of free discussion, may imprison or deport its honest and courageous thinkers who voice views distasteful to current majority opinion, and may falsify the teaching given in its schools to flatter the national ego and belittle other nations. A unity so maintained ends in national decadence, and renders unspiritual the life of the people, for liberty is indispensable to spirituality.

Nationalism's other necessity is autonomy to make its own political and social experiments. Every nation insists rightly on its sovereignty. Without freedom from foreign constraint and interference it cannot produce its distinctive contribution to the commonweal of the race. Nationalists in subject peoples are constantly in protest against governments which to them do not represent the national character. But there is a limit to the number of independent nations which, with profit to themselves and the world, can simultaneously pursue their self-determining ways, and in an earth as intimately interconnected as ours every nation's sovereignty must be subordinated to the common interest of mankind. There is a community of nations, more and more coming to self-consciousness, and only as a people dedicates itself to seek the welfare of that fellowship is it a spiritual nation.

History is witness that nations are not fixed and enduring entities. They are continually in flux. At the moment some groups are loudly clamoring for independent nationhood, and others are at pains to justify their inclusion of elements who wish to be free or annexed to a neighboring nation. In the past wars have been the usual means of changing national groupings; and any attempt in the interest of peace to stabilize the present number and extent of nations is fraught with peril to the development of the race. A nation carrying on a distinctive "experiment in living"[12] (to borrow a phrase of Professor Hocking's), which it cannot do except as an independent state, ought to have the chance to make its case at the bar of the judgment of mankind. Nations or primitive tribes who cannot at present maintain their independent statehood may have spiritual contributions of the utmost value, and there should be some means by which they too can be guaranteed by the collective judgment of the world such measure of autonomy within a larger whole as shall enable them to develop their own culture. The value to the world of a nation or tribe is not to be measured alone by its physical power to assert and defend itself, although vigor is an element in spirituality, but also by the distinctive quality of life which the group creates. The spiritual society of nations needs its

Bezalels and Stephens and Barnabases, as well as its Samsons. Hence to outlaw war is a step toward the creation of that society; and gradually means of common counsel must evolve, by which, without recourse to arms, the requisite changes and adaptations in political arrangements can be made to enable nations and tribes within nations to be their corporate spiritual selves.

We can estimate a nation's spirituality roughly by its attitude toward its own people and toward other nations. To what degree is it dedicated to the effort to render the national heritage for body, mind, and soul accessible to all of its inhabitants? Is there a chance for all of them to be physically well nourished, æsthetically enriched, intellectually equipped, socially enlarged, so that if they have it in them they can attain the spirituality of our four types? Is there scope for individual initiative so that divine promptings may show themselves in new ways? Are there elements in the population, deprived by their birth or color or other handicap for which they are not responsible, from participating fully in the national life? Are the nation's goods limited to favored groups, or is its "joy in widest commonalty shared"? Is there tolerance, so that its citizens think and speak freely, however widely they dissent from those who at the moment are dominant in government or in education, provided only they do not provoke to violence? Is the nation consecrated to furnish all its people life abundant?

And is the nation friendly and outgoing toward other nations? Does it recognize that, while their "experiments in living" differ from its own, they may have worth for mankind? Has it corporate imagination to appreciate the feelings of another people? Does it habitually think of itself as one of a community of nations, with an obligation so to order its affairs, to carry on its industry and commerce, to frame its politics and laws, to voice its opinions on the affairs of other nations and on the public concerns of humanity, that it promotes justice and goodwill, and does not exploit or injure any other people? Is there alive in its soul a sense of oneness with all men in the common experiment of human life, and does the nation dedicate itself to share the burdens and to foster the well-being of mankind?

Many hold this attempt quixotic. Nations have been and are predatory groups animated by economic self-interest and hallowing in their corporate dealings a spirit which a majority of their citizens would condemn in personal relations. Within they are torn by class warfare, in which, however covered up by pious hypocrisies, the few exploit the many. Self-styled realists deem it a sentimental dream to attempt to build out of these egotistic groups a community of nations, ruled by reason and conscience instead of by force and cunning. Some of them who outlaw war, still assert that an intensification of the class struggle within nations is the sole method to coerce the privileged to part with their economic and social advantages and to end outmoded conventions which spawn snobbery and servility. They declare that no privileged group ever gave up its power except under pressure, and that no oppressed group ever won its rights save by compulsion.

This is to despair of leavening society by spiritual means. It is to confine the transforming potency of Christ and the effectiveness of his methods to individuals and to sanction rougher means for correcting group relations. But unspiritual methods never produce spiritual results and cannot bring to pass the spiritual commonwealth. Unquestionably men in masses—in families or communities, in classes or nations or races, even in churches—seem less spiritually susceptible than as individuals. Most of the cruelty and brutality of the world is due not to hard-hearted villains, but to well-meaning unimaginative folk who cannot see the wrong caused by the group to which they belong and whose standards they conscientiously observe. Our worst sins are collective iniquities in which we unwittingly participate. What a city does in distorting the spirits of its citizens or in shutting finer things out of sight, what a nation by its self-centeredness permits to happen at the other side of the globe, what a class or race by maintaining its traditions evokes in another class or race—these by the numbers involved are the major tragedies of human relations. Men and women may be ethicized, but social groups seem hopeless.

But from the outset the Christian propaganda contemplated bringing social groups under the sway of the Spirit: "Go ye into all the world, and make all the *nations* disciples." Men are molded and permeated by the homes and communities and peoples to which they belong. And Christianity would supply them with an environment that imbues them with the spirit of Christ. When a state is truculent, its citizens become quarrelsome in their dealings with one another. When a race is looked down upon, its members compensate themselves by petty tyrannies over weaker folk of their own kind. If a family fosters friendship in the community, its sons and daughters are mutually considerate. And since everyone of us is kinsman and citizen, a man is frustrated in his public service by a selfish family and in an egotistical nation his patriotism is forced into hostility to the mind of his fellow-countrymen. The tension between the individual and the group to which he is bound by most sacred ties produces life's bitterest sorrows. There was no more intelligent patriot and understanding churchman in his Jerusalem than Stephen, and the leaders of nation and church stoned him to death. But Christianity rests upon the confidence that spiritual acts or martyrdoms beget spiritual responses. There is always some Saul among the bystanders, to become the apostle of a world-wide spiritual Israel—the Christian Church. The Spirit of God in a Stephen is the Spirit immanent, though imprisoned, in all, partially triumphing in some, and waiting for further stimulus to become the dominant motive.

And this is no less true of social groups than of individuals. A nation whose purposes are so fair that they are frankly stated can count on awakening confidence and evoking coöperation from parties in all civilized lands. A group which cannot justify its privileges by pointing to corresponding services rendered the body politic is already on the road to surrendering them. Men in communities feel themselves under obligation to the same principles which they accept for their private relations, although there are obvious differences in the application of these principles. A small spiritual minority cannot hurry an unspiritual population to a course for which they are unready, nor should an unspiritual remnant prevent a nation from enacting its best insights in its policies and legislation. The man who dedicates himself to the divine ideal for home and community and country, and pursues it by the spiritual means of persuasion, teaching, example, can be sure of awakening dormant enthusiasms and finding comrades, because the Spirit in him is the Spirit of the Father of mankind. To distrust spiritual means for achieving the spiritual society is to lack faith in the living God.

Already we have been treating a third and the most important social unit whose spirituality or want of it affects its members—the Christian Church. By the Church we mean that divine and human society, organized in various communions, in which Christ is the recognized head. It is divine not only in the sense that it originated in the act of God in the birth and death and resurrection of Jesus, but also that its members acknowledge themselves chosen to its fellowship by him. It is human in that it is composed of sinning and errant mortals. The one mark of the true Church, as the one sure token of the Christian, is the possession of the Spirit of Christ: *ubi Spiritus, ibi Ecclesia.*

This society is catholic or universal and supplies those who belong to it with a fellowship which transcends frontiers of race and nation and class. Its members are citizens of the various states in which they live, and must be faithful to their civic obligations. But they possess a supreme loyalty to Christ, and a comradeship in him with fellow-believers which is a closer tie than that which links them to non-Christian fellow citizens. By so much as the heritage of the Christian Church is richer than the national inheritance of any people, Christians of different nations or races have more in common than have believer and non-believer of the same land or race.

Inasmuch as the Church is essentially a fellowship, all divisions which so break its solidarity as to hinder its members from access to all its wealth in convictions and ideals, in worship and service, are schisms impoverishing the individual churchman, stunting the growth of the divine society, and thwarting its enrichment of the world. The Church needs enough outward expression of its unity to keep vigorous in all its members the sense of oneness with fellow-believers everywhere. And it needs sufficient liberty to allow individuals or groups within it to attain their full spiritual stature and exercise freely their spiritual gifts. Barnabas fostered its unity when he welcomed penitent Saul of Tarsus and the Gentile disciples at Antioch; Stephen laid down his life for liberty when he strove to lead the Jewish Church into the fuller light of Christ. The problem is always to maintain both the unity and the freedom of the Spirit. Only in the Church where a Christian can pray and work in genuine fellowship with all Christians, and where he can freely utter and carry out what God prompts him to say and do, does he develop fully in spirituality. Happily the bringing to fruition in our earth of such a Christian Church is not our responsibility only. It will come of God's inspiration and our responsive coöperation.

When one of the bridges which now connect Manhattan with Long Island was being built, the workmen, seeking to lay the base of a supporting tower in the bottom of the East River, discovered that years before a stone-laden scow had sunk at that spot and was deeply embedded in the mud. Divers were sent down, and managed to pass chains under the scow, and these were attached to tugs which tried to raise it; but in vain. One of the engineers conceived the plan of mooring two canal barges at low tide directly above the scow, fastening the chains to them, and waiting for the help of the Atlantic Ocean. When the tide rose, flooding up the bay from the great deep, slowly but surely it lifted the scow, and left the bridge-builders free to lay their foundation.

Bridge-building seems an apt parable of the task before this generation. There are new spiritual unities to be brought to conscious and efficient life in enduring homes, in international fellowship, in a comradeship of races and classes, in a comprehensive Church which shall embrace the whole household of Christian faith. Such bridges will not obliterate the lines indicating distinct units and assuring them their needful freedom, but will open to them more inclusive and enriching fellowship. And bridge-building is no easy task. We cannot minimize the obstacles in habits and thoughts and feelings, in ancient and deep-seated prejudices and suspicions, in intractable human selfishness. Our most strenuous efforts and most potent man-made contrivances are of themselves unavailing. But there is a unity and a liberty of the Spirit. We must consecrate our utmost strength and skill and mind and heart to the undertaking assigned our age. And beyond these we can wait confidently on God's Spirit, moving with the vast and mighty sweep of an ocean tide, through our endeavors to lift the obstacles and bind those whom he wills to make one.

VI

WHAT DO YOU MEAN BY "GOD"?

THE QUESTION WAS PUT BY A TYPICAL REPRESENTATIVE of the contemporary intelligentsia, a younger member of an academic faculty. "What do you mean by God? You modern Christians make your Deity assume as many forms as the fabled Proteus. Sometimes you speak of him as though he were the creative Life of the cosmos, and sometimes as though he were a Ruler above it. Sometimes you repeat the ancient legend, found in many primitive faiths, that he became man, and call a Galilean Peasant 'God'; again you bid men share Jesus' own faith in the Deity he worshiped. Sometimes you make God a Person; at other times a society of persons—Three in One. You presume that you 'know God'; well, then, why do you never tell us plainly who this Being is?"

Christian believers may seem a tantalizing combination of positiveness and vagueness. They speak of God with assurance; and are indefinite about him. But there is a similar mixture of certainty and mystery in our thought and speech about other major factors in life. We are confident of the existence of light; we count upon it in numberless ways; we can give an impressive list of vital services which it performs. But physicists are still inquiring what light is and hesitate to frame a definition of it. At times they speak of it as a form of motion, and at times as a quantum to be measured in tons per annum received by the earth. We know that persons exist; we know that they play all-important roles in our lives; and we can talk endlessly of what they mean to us as kindred and friends, neighbors and fellow-workers. But psychologists and philosophers are still exploring what personality is, and a completely satisfactory description of it is still to seek. Religious folk have no doubt that God is; in him they live and move and have their being; they can itemize a vast number of meanings God has for them. But the most clear-thinking saints are still following on to know him, and their every thought and word of him is no more than a fragmentary suggestion of what he is.

A modern French thinker said: "Le Dieu défini est le Dieu fini." Another brilliant Frenchman, the chief theologian of the Reformation, who has been called far too precise and dogmatic in his assertions about Deity, John Calvin, wrote:

"God treats sparingly of his essence. His essence is

indeed incomprehensible by us. Let us therefore willingly leave to God the knowledge of himself." [1]

The foremost of English divines, Richard Hooker, uttered a similar warning:

> "Dangerous it were for the feeble brain of man to wade into the doings of the Most High; whom although to know be life, and joy to make mention of his name; yet our soundest knowledge is, to know that we know him not as indeed he is, neither can know him; and our safest eloquence concerning him is our silence, when we confess without confession, that his glory is inexplicable, his greatness above our capacity and reach." [2]

We may be thankful that Hooker did not confine himself to his "safest eloquence," for we should be the poorer for some profound religious insights and many pages of stately English prose. But all the first-rate devout thinkers agree that God transcends every human attempt to portray him. We can never *comprehend* him, but we can more and more *apprehend* him.

What, then, do we mean by "God"? One hears intelligent men saying that they can believe in God, provided they are not asked to describe him. Such totally indefinite belief reminds one of the chart with which the Bellman provided his crew in Lewis Carroll's poem:

> A large map representing the sea
>   Without the least vestige of land.
>
> Other maps are such shapes with their island and capes!
>   But we've our brave captain to thank

[So the crew would protest] that he's bought us the best—
A perfect and absolute blank.[3]

Vital religion is a matter of clear thinking, no less than of ardent feeling and conscientious life; and, granted that any attempt to describe the Christian conviction is tentative and fractional, there is value in trying to be as exact as one can. Let us return to the first lecture, and recall that in answer to the query, Where can we start in our religious thinking? we began with man's tacit recognition of a Factor in the universe working for good and an Ideal of goodness to which he feels obliged to be loyal.

By "God," then, we mean that creative Spirit behind and in the universe to whom we are indebted for what is given us and for the capacities by which we can add to the creation. There is an epitaph on one of the last pages of the last collection of verse published by Thomas Hardy, which begins with the lines:

I never cared for Life: Life cared for me,
And hence I owed it some fidelity.

In his *Dynasts* he had pictured the ultimate force in the universe as indifferent Will:

Like a knitter drowsed
Whose fingers play in skilled unmindfulness,
The Will has woven with an absent heed
Since life first was.

But that was an impression gained from observation of

history in the large. Thinking of his own career, the elderly poet is in another mood. Life is prior to us, and *cares* for us, and therefore holds a claim upon us.

A contemporary Indian philosopher, Professor Radhakrishnan, makes a like affirmation:

> "When we sink back into the inmost core of our lives, we are compelled, whether we like it or not, to accept the universe. Atheism is contrary to the ultimate instinct of life. That life is good and is to be made the most of is the act of faith, the unanalyzable ultimate for which no reasons could be given." [4]

Biblical religion, much more explicity, confesses that we are dependent upon and obliged to the Source of life for the goods about and within us. "It is he that hath made us, and not we ourselves; we are his people," is the fundamental faith of the Old Testament; and the New repeats it: "To us there is one God, the Father, of whom are all things, and we unto him."

To be sure when we identify God with the Source of that which seems good to us, we recall that we men are not his sole concern. He makes the rain to fall, as Job was told, "on a land where no man is." We adore God in the inscrutable mystery of the universe which yields no meaning to us whatsoever. All in the cosmos and in history which cannot be interpreted in human values need not be chaos. The whole purpose of God cannot be captured and phrased in terms intelligible to us. God is other than man and his thoughts are not our thoughts. But we believe that he whom we acknowledge and revere as the Wellspring of life, even of its to us tantalizing riddles and unfathomable secrets, is the God who has made himself known as our Kinsman, caring for us and claiming our devotion.

This obligation masters us in an Ideal from which we cannot withhold our allegiance. Granted that the Ideal has changed with man's developing conscience, and that there is no such thing as a universally acknowledged standard of goodness, but rather a series of insights by the seers of the race, once their insight is proclaimed it meets with response. "We needs must love the highest when we see it." This progressively discovered, or rather progressively revealed, Perfection to which we are constrained to conform, is what we mean by "God."

Sometimes we think of the Ideal as *truth.* The universe is fashioned and develops according to principles which we discover. We speak of them as "facts." They compel our assent. We call them stubborn or imperious. Browning writes in *Asolando:*

> In flowed
> Ever-resistless fact:
> No more than the passive clay
> Disputes the potter's act,
> Could the whelmed mind disobey
> Knowledge the cataract.

Through the cumulative impression made upon us by these data we come to realize the structure of the universe, and find our aptest symbol to explain it in Mind. We picture God to ourselves in terms of intelligence.

Sometimes the Ideal claims us as *beauty*. There is in nature, in music, in art, in literature, in the acts and characters of men that which charms us. We cannot refuse our admiration. This loveliness in landscape or poem or holy life satisfies us with a sense of blessedness. An architect, who underwent a sudden tragic bereavement, published a sonnet, in which he pictures Beauty saying:

> He that keeps faith with me will surely find
> My substance in the shadows on the deep,
> My spirit in the courage that men keep
> Though all the stars burn out and Heaven goes blind.
> When sorrow smites thee, look! my joy is near,
> Flashing like sunlight on a falling tear.[5]

Men thus oriented to life worship God, the altogether Lovely, whose will they fulfill in interpreting and embodying in various forms the Beautiful.

Sometimes the Ideal confronts us as *right*. Akin to the facts which make up the fabric of existence, and to "the iron laws of beauty," are the principles of justice and goodwill by which men live together in harmony. The particular forms these take vary as human society evolves. "Time makes ancient good uncouth," but the soul of goodness—honesty, kindness, consideration, justice, love—lives on. He must be blind indeed who does not see a moral force flamingly present in history. Nations disregard brotherhood, rely on force and cunning, strive to grab land or raw materials or commercial advantages, and a conflagration, such as the World War, destroys lives by the million and leaves a continent in penury. A nation's inhabitants set personal gain before the commonweal, forget the weak, indulge in speculation, worship pleasure, live loose to the marriage-tie and to civic obligation, and the wages of sin are paid in economic depression and in the misery of the unemployed. This is the wrath of God in human affairs—the vindication of the righteousness of love.

The sunlight filters so softly through the atmosphere in our temperate zone and is so beneficent to life that we accept Wordsworth's metaphor "hurtless light."[6] When we witness an eclipse, it surprises us that at the moment of totality jagged flames shoot out, disclosing the fiery planet which the sun is. Eclipses in the world's life, which to many appear to blot God out altogether, show him a consuming fire. If we stop to think about it, the daily sunshine is destructive to germs of disease, and thus brings and conserves health. He in whom mankind lives is holy love.

And as with society, so with the individual, it is this moral factor with which we must finally reckon. Conscience pummels and pounds us. It wakes us in the night with a start; it dogs our steps by day. It knocks us down and leaves us on our faces in the dirt, ready to let any passer-by trample us. Again it lifts us up, and sends us off after a purpose as lofty and unattainable as a star in the sky. People may think us mad, but this quest grips us. If we are faithless to it, conscience digs spurs into us and lays on the whip. If we follow with our might, there is an inward peace worth more to us than all the plaudits of a world. This righteousness is God, his most intimate and compelling presence within us.

In that penetrating study of three generations *The Forsyte Saga,*[7] his son says to Jolyon Forsyte:

> "Do you believe in God, Dad?"
> "What do you mean by God?" he said; "there are two irreconcilable ideas of God. There's the unknowable Creative Principle—one believes in That. And there's the Sum of Altruism in man—naturally one believes in That."
> "I see. That leaves out Christ, doesn't it?"
> "Jolyon stared. Christ the link between the two ideas! The sublime poem of Christ's life was man's attempt to join these two irreconcilable conceptions of God. And since the Sum of human altruism was as much part of the unknowable Creative Principle as anything else in Nature and the Universe, a worse link might have been chosen after all."

Christians start with this link. The supreme religious fact for them is Jesus. He evokes our trust, our loyalty, our adoration. He masters our reasons as truth, interpreting for us the ultimate meaning of life —a fellowship like his with God and man. His initial role is that of a teacher. He would be puzzled by the numerous company in our time who admire his idealism and courage, but consider him deluded in his dominant conviction concerning God. The world keeps trying other ways of life, for his is so difficult, but repeated disasters leave us haunted with the conviction that he is right. His insights are correct.

He fascinates us by the beauty of his life and the sublimity of his sacrifice on the cross. He has a charm which makes his portrait on the pages of the evangelists the masterpiece of literature. One of the early Greek Fathers declares:

> "He is so lovely, as to be alone loved by us, whose hearts are set on true beauty." [8]

His figure towers above us in moral grandeur, leaving us "lost in wonder, love, and praise."

He lays hold of our consciences; searches us; abases us. He constrains us, and we yield to him, and are exalted with a sense of forgiveness and admission to partnership with him in the purpose of God. But although he calls us friends, we never feel ourselves his equals. Those who speak of their companionship with him in terms that suggest "chumminess" seem blasphemous. He is so high above us in his faith and love that we bow before him.

In this Man of Nazareth the living God unveils himself most clearly to us. He deals with us transformingly. He gives us light and strength and life; he gives us himself—we can say nothing less. We cannot call Christ's life, as Galsworthy does, only "man's attempt." It seems to us a joint attempt—God's attempt to reveal himself and man's attempt to fulfill God's will. And because there is in Christ's life this combined effort, he is for us God's utmost gift and man's perfect achievement. In Jesus we possess the disclosure of the creative Spirit of the universe to whom we owe all things, and the Ideal for which we must live, and if need be die.

Many who accept Christ as "the Sum of Altruism in man" would rebel at Galsworthy's proposal to link him with "the unknowable Creative Principle." Is not life terrible with tragedy? Think of diseases that rack with agony and disasters that overwhelm millions. Is not the cosmos bleakly indifferent to heroic struggles for justice and pitiable pleas for love? Are not men so made that we seem inevitably heartless and cruel to our fellow-creatures and often fiendish to those whom we think we love? How can we make the devoted Christ the symbol of the ultimate Force in the universe?

Galsworthy felt the difficulty of making this identification and called the conceptions of the human Ideal and the cosmic Principle irreconcilable. But Christians mastered by the love of Christ are forced to a leap of faith. Christ's God is so good that he must be true. They are prepared to hazard everything on the assumption that he is Lord of heaven and earth. And as they live to make love supreme in human society and face the seemingly uncaring cosmos with trust that kindred Love rules it, they discover that such love creates satisfactory human relations, and such trust renders them conquerors over pain and separation and disappointment and apparent defeat. There is no logic by which they can prove that Christlike Love dominates the universe. It may seem madness to suppose it. In the eyes of the worldly-wise they are fools. To themselves they are "fools for Christ's sake." And under his spell they discover that they can live and die triumphantly. They have never convinced men merely by the cogency of their arguments; but they have demonstrated in life and death a power men could not but covet. They can vindicate their faith as the victory which overcometh the world. That vindication is far from complete. The evidence will not all be in until the kingdoms of this world—kingdoms of industry and politics, races and individuals—are brought under the sway of Christ. Meanwhile, however, the Christian, by what he does and in what he bears by faith, can demonstrate that in Christ he has the link binding the ideal to cosmic power. "Who is he that overcometh the world, but he that believeth that Jesus is the Son of God?"

If, then, a Christian be asked, "What do you mean by 'God'?" the main emphasis of his reply is: "The Spirit over and in the world, the quality of whose being is seen in Jesus of Nazareth." The forms in which God comes to us may be Protean (to employ our questioner's metaphor), but he is everywhere and always Christlike. We do not acknowledge anything Divine which is at variance with the life and cross of

Jesus; and wherever we catch sight of aught akin to him, there we worship a glimpse of the face of God.

Our questioner complained because at times Christians address a Galilean Peasant as God after the manner of primitive legends of deities appearing in human form, and at other times bid men share the religion by which Jesus lived.

In our thought of Jesus we begin with the Man. He stands before us on the pages of the Gospels with "uplooking trust"—the Chief of believers. He worships an august and devoted God. The false views of him against which the early Christians protested were denials of his humanity. We recognize behind the Church which grew out of his work, and the writings in which adoring followers enshrined his memory, an historic figure sharing the life of his time and place. His outlook on the cosmos, his forms of thought, his language, are those of a first-century Palestinian Jew. His religious insights, his purpose for mankind, his method of achieving it, his character, transcend time, and make him the contemporary of the successive ages. We begin by following him into his faith in God. This faith is not altogether original with him: it was the faith of his people. It is difficult to point to a single item in his thought of God that is entirely novel. But his intimacy with God made his fellowship with him so distinctive that a devout and zealous Jewish believer like Saul of Tarsus, after he became a Christian, spoke habitually of "the God and Father of our Lord Jesus Christ." We find God clearly in the response from the unseen which answered the faith of Jesus, or in that approach from the unseen which evoked the character of Jesus.

Jesus' preferred name for him was "Father." Like all language, it is a symbol. Reared in a Jewish home, it expressed for him authority and affection. Jesus revered and trusted God. Despite current criticisms that it fosters infantilism, the name most aptly fits One before whom we are as little children. So unconventional a Christian as George Meredith wrote:

> "I hold to the word 'Father.' No young child can take the meaning of 'Spirit.' You must give him a concrete form or he will not put an idea in what he is uttering. He must address somebody. Later, when he throws off his childishness, he will, if you are watching and assisting him, learn to see that he prayed to no false impersonation in addressing an invisible 'Father.' "[9]

Perhaps there was more to Jesus in this symbol. He employed human relations as metaphors of spiritual kinship. By "Father" he stressed that his was a derived life, drawing from God his purposes and interests and energies. God's paternity to him was not only a past event but a continuing process. By his obedience he let God father his life and death.

So completely was this the case that his followers found in him, particularly as they looked back in perspective upon his figure, the unveiling of the God to whom he prayed. They were strict monotheists, believing that God is one, but they found no incongruity in thinking of their Master as at God's right hand. Indeed they could think of him nowhere else. So intimate had seemed his fellowship with the Most High, that they associated God and Jesus in the same thought. The Being whom they had adored in Jesus' company, praying with him "Our Father," they saw mirrored in the life and cross of this Man whose friends they were.

What we call the "divinity" or "deity" of Jesus is not something he taught about himself. It was the spontaneous outgrowth of his disciples' impression of his filial fellowship with God and of their discovery in him of the God to whom he led them. Nor are we concerned to assert it because we wish to say something about Jesus. What he is speaks for itself. But we wish to make plain what we mean by divinity, by God. This Man, the distinctive flavor of whose life we know through the company of followers he created and his impress on them, defines for us the God we worship.

Apart from Jesus, God remains vague. With the Old Testament we may picture him as the embodiment of virtues, saying God is truth, righteousness, justice, faithfulness, or even God is love; or we may pile up similes likening him to a strong fortress, the shelter of a great rock, a spring of living water, a lasting home; we may fetch metaphors from human relations and call him King, Guide, Father, Husband, Friend; but all these nouns, however rich in association, lack the distinctive quality which he has for us when we address him as the God and Father of Jesus Christ.

At a meeting where Jewish and Christian clergymen were discussing their common task of leading folk into fellowship with the living God, one of the rabbis remarked that he envied his Christian colleagues the definiteness of the idea of God which they brought to their people through their use of the Prophet of Nazareth as a symbol for Deity. Jesus is our vivid and moving metaphor for God. The Divine Word made flesh becomes incalculably more intelligible, more appealing, more cogent.

It has always been so. Centuries ago Augustine tells us that in his search for God, he had caught sight of him through Platonic philosophy and had been ravished by his beauty, but received no permanent nourishment. He compares himself to a man with an appetite, but unable to find strengthening food. This he found in the Man Christ Jesus, "the Word made flesh." [10] More than a thousand years later an Augustinian monk, Martin Luther, made a similar discovery, and breaking with the formal conception of God current in the Church of his day, insisted that God deals with us transformingly only when we let him give himself to us in Christ. "Anything that one imagines of God apart from Christ is only useless thinking and vain idolatry." [11]

We say that Jesus *defines* God for us; and we add at once, but does not *confine* him. This human Life reveals all of God that a human life can contain; but there is more in the God of the universe. The Church did not discard the Old Testament when Christians confessed a fuller embodiment of the Divine in Jesus. The insights of Israel's prophets, in which Jesus was nourished, remain valid. So, too, are the insights by which believers in other religious traditions have lived. No Christian would disparage the spiritual vision of Gautama or of Confucius or of Mohammed, or of any other seer who has enriched his fellows in faith and righteousness. Our God has not left himself anywhere without witness. We acknowledge his revelations to men of all races, as they were able to perceive him. We test them for ourselves by their congruity with the disclosure in Jesus.

Nor do we limit God's Self-revelation to the religious and ethical life of men. He is Truth and Beauty, as well as Goodness. Interpreters of the physical universe, of human history, and priests "of the wonder and bloom of the world" in art and music and letters, enlarge our fellowship with him. There are no frontiers within which God's life is bounded. He is

> That Light whose smile kindles the universe,
> That Beauty in which all things work and move.[12]

The centre of our fellowship with him is in Jesus, the circumference stretches off to infinite horizons.

Some Christians identify Jesus with God in a way foreign to his own thought of his derived life and mediating task. He is the Son, not the Father; the Way, not the End. When the statement is made unqualifiedly that Jesus is God, the historic teaching of the Church is as much distorted as when with similar finality it is asserted that Jesus is man. We do not say that a bay *is* the ocean because the water in both is of the same saltiness, and the tides in the one ebb and flow in unison with those in the other. We should not identify them, even were there but one such bay. There is a unique Self-revelation of God in Jesus; he is God incarnate; but he is not the entire Godhead. If at the climax of a Gospel he is hailed by a penitent convinced disciple, "My Lord and my God," the same evangelist calls "gods" those to whom the divine message came. If an apostle declares that in Jesus "dwelleth the fullness of the Godhead bodily," he also prays that Christians "may be filled unto all the fullness of God." Another New Testament writer views him as "the firstborn among many brethren," and still another finds the fulfillment of Jesus' mission in rendering his followers "partakers of the divine nature." In Jesus we know the quality of God's life: God is never unlike Jesus; and there is no end to the Self-giving of God to his children, nor of his Self-disclosure in his universe. The Christian hopes for a perfected society where God shall be "all in all."

Our questioner found a discrepancy in the Christian presentation of God now as the creative Life of the cosmos, now as a Ruler above it. Obviously words like "above" and "within" are not used spatially when connected with Spirit. To faith God controls the universe to the extent that despite refractory elements in it his good purpose will be achieved, and he pervades it, ceaselessly toiling to fashion it after his heart.

Picturing God as "above" the world is a way of distinguishing between God and the world. He is to us more than nature or humanity. He stands over against man and his world in his holy love. God is what we and our fellows are not, and we are humbled before him. He is also other than what we find in nature. We do not rise "through nature to God," we ascend "from nature's God up to the Christian's God"—the God revealed in Jesus.[13] Not only human society but the whole creation is imperfect and travailing to bring forth a different world—a world reborn after the likeness of our holy God. There is no place in a Christian's heart for complacency with himself or for satisfaction with things as they are. God looms above us, the Most High, and the contrast between his character and ours is clear in such a clash as the tragedy at Golgotha. We and he are so unlike that where we dominate he is murdered. Nevertheless he lives and conquers. Again and again in history God seems to manifest himself in doom, judging faithless men and condemning social systems which foster injustice. But these dooms are the birth-pangs in which something diviner is born into our world. In the evolution of our planet novelties have emerged, like life and mind, and like finer ideals which put to shame current standards. To the Christian these novelties come from God, or rather in them God comes and discloses more of himself. Such an emergence or invasion was Jesus, and there have been many other advents of God in history and in the experience of individuals. The constant prayer of the Church is "Come"—*Veni, sancte Spiritus.* It is not a prayer offered by those who question God's presence within them: they confess his indwelling. He is already penetrating their souls and steadily pressing them toward goodness. But they also view him far aloft in his perfectness, and keep longing for his further coming to transform and fill them with his love. And with each advent they know themselves both blest and judged, possessing and lacking, satisfied and doomed to more acute discontent.

At the moment the latter mood is dominant. A world with plenty available for all and with millions in want seems a world under judgment, a world condemned. But to believers it is condemned that it may be redeemed and enter into diviner life. We are in the midst of an earth-wide advent, if only we know the day of our visitation. Our disgust and longing are the open gates of heaven out through which God is entering our time to bring to those who will receive him a more thoughtful justice and a kindlier fellowship.

Nor do we consider that in all these advents so far God has arrived completely. He always towers beyond the as-yet-dreamed. We have glimpses of his transcendent kingdom gleaming afar. We look for further ingressions that he may come to his own and be manifest in "realms where the air we breathe is love." It is this difference in God by which he is "above" us which both abases and uplifts us in hope.

Picturing God as "within" the world, and especially within the spirits of men, is a way of saying that he works through, and not apart from, the processes of nature and the thoughts of his children. We draw no line between the natural and the supernatural, between human and superhuman activities. We believe that we are divinely led not when we discard our own judgment and the counsel of our wisest advisers, and depend upon uncriticized "hunches" or upon some irrational device, like the casting of lots or the toss of a coin. "The spirit of man is the candle of the Lord." Our brains and consciences, and the insights of the most ethically sensitive, are the means through which his mind is opened to us. And we insist that "within" and "above" are one, that God is both resident in our existing knowledge, and that, when we wait upon him seeking light, there is an advent of God to direct us. We express it in such phrases as, "It came over me," "It was borne in upon me." This is not to fall back upon the irrational, but to employ our intelligence to the utmost, looking to God for enlightenment and for confirmation or non-confirmation of our judgment.

In our decisions there is often an element which seems to go beyond our reasoning. It is the response of our whole being to the gleam of a peremptory obligation or of a beckoning hope. We do not see more than a step of our way ahead. We cannot forecast whither we are being taken, or what issues will ensue from our work. We are in the hands of a Wiser than we; our minds go with him so far as they can go, but there is an inward compulsion which carries us beyond our ability to foresee.

> The best men, doing their best,
> Know peradventure least of what they do:
> Men usefullest i' the world are simply used.[14]

This living in the Spirit delivers from anxiety, self-consciousness, and conceit.

Similarly we believe that in our efforts to create a better world God works. This gives us an assurance that the outcome will be above aught we anticipate or propose. Much is being said to-day about a planned society. No Christian, who believes that the Spirit of God inspires the conscientious endeavors of men to rear the most just and friendly commonwealth of which they can conceive, belittles the visions, or even the blue-prints, of these fraternal utopias. But suppose the wisdom of the total proletariat of all lands, or of the so-called economic experts, or of those acknowledged to possess the most acute social consciences, could be pooled, and a new world designed, this would not be the kingdom of God.

As Christians we welcome the dreams of seers, and are open-minded to the more prosaic proposals of social engineers. But we scrutinize them in the light of the high and holy God, and view their attempt at human justice and fellowship before the judgment-seat of his love. While we can and must work for measures which promise social betterment as in line with his will, we can never think them absolute. At best they will be crude approximations of his purpose. Hence whether to maintain things as they are or to establish a more equalitarian order, we oppose rigid political regimentation, which curtails freedom of thought and speech, and impedes orderly change. Where the Spirit of the Lord is, there is liberty; and liberty is the atmosphere favorable to the Spirit's further revelation. We believe in the use of the wisdom offered by the social sciences, or supplied by past or current experiments in comradely life. And through and beyond this wisdom, we would be led by the mind of Christ, and looking for his contemporary guidance in the application of that mind to present situations.

Then the outcomes to-morrow and some decades hence have a chance of surpassing our expectations. Through men dedicated to the reign of God and his righteousness the indwelling Spirit can bring to pass divine purposes. So comes to us

> from the unknown
> And inaccessible solitudes of being,
> The rushing of the sea-tides of the soul;
> And inspirations, that we deem our own,
> Are some divine foreshadowing and foreseeing
> Of things beyond our reason or control.[15]

There is no contradiction between a God who is Ruler over the world and creative Life within it. We wish a God-made world, but we do not think that he will create it entirely without us. We see his Spirit moving in the adaptive life of the cosmos, and supremely in the aspirations of men for fellowship one with another and with him. To consecrate ourselves under the lordship of Jesus to seek a society moved by his faith and love, is to further a commonwealth—whether it come on this planet or in realms beyond our ken—a commonwealth so far exceeding our anticipations that we shall hail it as the city whose builder and maker is God.

Our questioner alleged another confusion in the Christian thought of God, in that at times we speak of him as a Person, and at other times as Three Persons.

In a previous lecture it has been made plain that in predicating personality of God we recognize "otherness" as well as a likeness to ourselves. We know of no personality who pervades a universe, "Centre and Soul of every sphere." We admit an altogether impassable difference between God and man. But personality is the highest emergent in the evolution of our world, and we dare not attribute less to its creative Spirit. Religious people find personal terms aptest to describe One who has fellowship with them. Even Hardy could not avoid such a term when he wrote: "Life *cared* for me." Further we see personality in various stages of development in this "vale of soul-making" from a primitive savage to a Plato or a Shakespeare, and in God doubtless it transcends aught man on earth can attain. We are germinal persons—tadpoles of persons (so to say). The evangelist who places on Jesus' lips the saying, "He that hath seen me hath seen the Father," makes him add: "The Father is greater than I." It is sometimes said that Jesus taught the humanness of God; but it is as true to say that he pointed up from man at his best to more and better in God. He contrasted the mind of God with the mind of man. He insisted on the superhumanness of God. While Christian faith has recognized a kinship of God with man, so that closest intercourse is possible, it acknowledges a permanent distinction. God and men will never be identical. He will remain other than we.

When Christians speak of Three Persons in the Godhead, "persons" do not mean personalities. The doctrine of the Trinity is an attempt, in terms of Greek philosophy, both to hold fast Jewish monotheism against pagan polytheism, and to sum up the rich Christian experience of God.

With Jesus his disciples came to speak of God oftenest as Father, and to live with him in filial trust and devotion. It was a reverent and worshipful fellowship with One whom they adored as the Most High, Lord of heaven and earth. Then, after Jesus' death and resurrection, they spoke of Jesus as Lord, thought of him on the throne of the universe, and saw reflected in him the God into whose fellowship he had led them. They did not deify him, and make him a second Divinity; they knew that through him God had disclosed himself to them, and given them life abundant. The critical study of the New Testament makes clear that neither Jesus himself nor his first interpreters thought of his life and death as a man's heroism, but as "an act of God wrought out in human flesh and blood." [16] After Jesus' physical departure, the Christian community found themselves possessed, empowered, guided, kindled. This Divine Presence they spoke of as God in them, or Christ in them, or the Spirit of God corporately shared by them. Long before a doctrine of the

Trinity was formulated, these Three were put together, for example, in the familiar benediction: "The grace of the Lord Jesus Christ, and the love of God, and the communion of the Holy Spirit, be with you all."

Doctrines, like dictionary definitions, are efforts to explain words which men have instinctively coined for their experiences. If you look up the Century Dictionary's description of the verb "to kiss," the lexicographer informs us that it is

> "to smack with the pursed lips (a compression of the closed cavity of the mouth by the cheeks giving a slight sound when the rounded contact of the lips with one another is broken)."

This is perhaps as accurate an account of the matter as can be written. It is unlikely, however, that any mother cons it in order to embrace her baby; or that a suitor studies it before proposing to the young woman whom he is wooing. Our response to God is as spontaneous as to our dearest. Only later, when we must tell others or make plain to ourselves whom we have found God to be, do we attempt descriptions and frame doctrines. Their value lies in forcing us to try to think precisely, and in consequence to live more intelligently with God. One of the profoundest students of comparative religion in our time, the late Professor George F. Moore, concluded his lectures on the birth and growth of religion with the sentence:

> "The intellectual victory of Christianity over all the rival salvations of the time was due to the fact that it alone offered not merely a way of salvation but a philosophy of salvation." [17]

Part of that philosophy was this doctrine.

Trinity or Triunity is, as Luther said, a "cold" word, a mathematical formula, not valuable in devout intercourse with God.[18] "Person" is the Latin translation of the Greek "hypostasis," and stands for something between personality and personification, in our modern use of those words. Theologians hesitated to employ it, aware of the peril of its being misunderstood. Augustine wrote:

> "Human utterance, in answer to the question, 'Why Three Persons?' truly labors under a great insufficiency. We do, however, speak of Three Persons, not in order that we may speak in such terms, but that we may not be silent." [19]

Nor is the conception of a trinity in God a unique Christian teaching. Greek philosophers adore Truth, Beauty, Goodness; and Hindu seers speak of the one God, who creates as Brahma, redeems as Vishnu, and judges as Siva. That other devout souls have come to this discovery of a threeness in Deity confirms our interpretation. But the distinctive quality of the Christian view of God is not his triunity, but his character. The figure of the historic Jesus makes the difference. St. Paul's familiar benediction begins not with

God, but with Jesus: "The grace of the Lord Jesus Christ, and the love of God." Chronologically speaking we may call the historic Jesus the First Person of the Trinity.

By calling God triune, then, we affirm first that he is one. We do not worship a triumvirate. We never say "They," but "He." We do not distinguish between fellowship with the Father, and fellowship with Christ, or with the Spirit. Nor can we assign functions or offices to the Spirit or to the Son distinct from those of the Father. The God with whom we have to do is always the Father, revealed in Jesus, spiritually present in the life of the community of his followers. He who sees Christ sees the Father and sees the Spirit. He who lives under the inspiration of the Spirit knows the Father and the Son. God is everywhere and invariably Christlike love.

And, second, we try by the doctrine to interpret the richness of God's Self-disclosure in the Christian Church. The doctrine, admittedly an inadequate formulation, is prized because it conserves this wealth.

> Some seek a Father in the heavens above;
> Some ask a human image to adore;
> Some crave a Spirit vast as life and love;
> Within Thy mansions we have all and more.[20]

If God is these Three to us, there is that in him to which our discoveries correspond, although it is beyond human powers to peer into the secrets of the Divine

Being. Luther warned of the unprofitableness of discussing what God does and thinks and is "by himself." [21] The purpose of the doctrine is intensely practical—not to tantalize our minds with puzzles for speculation, but to furnish us with the results of God's revelation to Christian saints, in order that with the fullness of their heritage we may live and labor with him in our day. Zwingli well said: "A Christian man's task is not to talk grandly of doctrines, but always to be doing hard and great things with God." *(Christiani hominis est non de dogmatis magnifica loqui, sed cum deo ardua semper et magna facere.*[22]*)*

Indeed the riches of Divine fellowship which the Christian Church has sought to interpret in this doctrine are intelligible only to those who in faith try to follow Jesus in establishing the reign of God. They know a Father's love; they rely on the redeeming grace of Christ; they let themselves be led and used by the indwelling Spirit. To them the pathos of life is that this God of such exhaustless meaning is not far from everyone of his children, and yet is so often ignored.

When oil was discovered in Oklahoma, two decades or more ago, a New York newspaper sent a reporter to write up the story. Among other things he told of an unusually productive well that had been sunk on the former property of an elderly couple, who had emigrated from North Carolina and taken up this land when it had been opened for settlement, and had eked out a scanty livelihood by farming. One day some men had come along and asked the woman for a drink from her well. She had been a little surprised to see them take some of the water away in a bottle. Later they had returned and made an offer for the farm which seemed liberal and was accepted. A pipe was driven down between the house and barn, and the quantity of the flow of oil was the talk of the neighborhood. The reporter told of seeing the old man and his wife leaning on a fence, watching the operation of the well, and of overhearing the woman say to her husband: "To think that we slaved here for years, and all this was at our doorstep, and we never knew it."

God, who means everything to those who trust him, is accessible to all men, eagerly waiting to give us the fullness of his life; but it is tragically possible to be preoccupied with other things, unaware of him, and to spend our days in poverty-stricken godlessness.

REFERENCES

CHAPTER I

1 — *The Life and Letters of Sir Edmund Gosse,* by Evan Charteris, p. 198 (Harper and Brothers)

2 — *Whitman,* by Emory Holloway, p. 42 (Alfred A. Knopf)

3 — *Beyond Life,* by James Branch Cabell (McBride Company)

4 — *The Interior* for January 10, 1901

5 — *Sestina of the Tramp Royal* in 1896

6 — To J. A. C. in *Rhymes and Rhythms* (Thomas B. Mosher)

7 — *Experience and Art,* by Joseph Wood Krutch, pp. 219 and 221 (Harrison Smith and Robert Haas)

8 — *Parleyings,* Prologue l. 246, and *A Grammarian's Funeral*

9 — *The Hermitage and Later Poems,* p. 24 (Houghton Mifflin Company)

10 — *Samuel Butler: A Memoir,* by Henry Festing Jones, Vol. II, p. 74 (Macmillan Company)

11 — *England,* by Wilhelm Dibelius, p. 482 (Harper and Brothers)

12 — *Belief Unbound,* by W. P. MONTAGUE, p. 1 (Yale University Press)

13 — *The Revolt of the Masses,* by JOSE ORTEGA Y GASSET, Eng. tr., p. 75 (W. W. Norton Company, Inc.)

14 — The Foundation of the French Academy, in *Aspects and Impressions,* by SIR EDMUND GOSSE, p. 165 (Charles Scribner's Sons)

15 — *Selected Letters,* edited by B. HOLLAND, p. 267 (E. P. Dutton and Company)

16 — *The Life and Letters of Leslie Stephen,* by F. W. MAITLAND, p. 256 (G. P. Putnam's Sons)

17 — *The Letters of Katherine Mansfield,* Vol. II, p. 389 (Alfred A. Knopf)

18 — *Id.,* p. 398

19 — Letter of December 2, 1796, in *The Life of Charles Lamb,* by E. V. LUCAS, p. 108 (Methuen and Company, Ltd.)

20 — *The Letters of Katherine Mansfield,* Vol. II, p. 403

21 — *The Worst Journey in the World,* by A. CHERRY GARRARD, Vol. II, p. 485 (Doran and Company)

22 — *Prayer,* by F. HEILER, Eng. tr., p. 262 (Oxford University Press)

23 — *Those Earnest Victorians,* by E. WINGFIELD STRATFORD, pp. 258 and 332 (Morrow Company)

24 — *The Epic of America,* by JAMES TRUSLOW ADAMS, p. 400 (Little, Brown and Company)

REFERENCES

CHAPTER II

1 — *Red Rust,* by Cornelia James Cannon (Little, Brown and Company)

2 — *The City of Dreadful Night,* by James Thomson (Kahoe and Spieth)

3 — *My Apprenticeship,* by Beatrice Webb, p. 95 (Longmans)

4 — *The Right to Be Happy,* by Dora Russell, pp. 101 and 241 (George Routledge and Sons, Ltd.)

5 — *Three Pairs of Silk Stockings,* by Panteleimon Romanof, Eng. tr., p. 224 (Scribners)

6 — *John Addington Symonds,* A Biography, by Horatio F. Brown, p. 317 (Scribners)

7 — *Philosophies,* by Sir Ronald Ross, pp. 21 and 53 (John Murray)

8 — From a newspaper interview. Similar expressions of faith are in Sir E. H. Shackleton, *The Heart of the Antarctic,* Vol. II, pp. 182, 211, and 217 (Heinemann)

9 — *The Autobiography of Henry M. Stanley,* p. 519 (Houghton Mifflin Company)

10 — *Exhortation to the Heathen,* Chap. XI in *The Ante-Nicene Fathers,* Vol. II, p. 203

11 — *The Apology of Aristides,* in the Additional Volume to the Ante-Nicene Christian Library, p. 227

12 — *The Brontës' Life and Letters,* by Clement Shorter, Vol. II, pp. 35, 36 (Scribners)

13 — *Abraham Lincoln,* by JOHN DRINKWATER, p. 24 (Houghton Mifflin Company)

14 — *Abraham Lincoln: A History,* by NICOLAY AND HAY, Vol. III, p. 291 (Century Company)

15 — Entry for May 21, 1854, *The Life and Works of the Earl of Shaftesbury,* by EDWIN HODDER, p. 494 (Cassell and Company, Ltd.)

16 — In the year 1867. *Ibid.,* p. 620

17 — *The Letters of William James,* Vol. II, p. 211 (The Atlantic Monthly Press)

18 — *Ibid.,* 213, 214

19 — *The Adams Family,* by JAMES TRUSLOW ADAMS, pp. 232, 233 (Little, Brown and Company)

CHAPTER III

1 — *Letters of Emily Dickinson,* edited by MABEL LOOMIS TODD, p. 257 (Harper and Brothers)

2 — *Song of Myself,* 46, in *Leaves of Grass*

3 — *The Letters of William James,* Vol. II, p. 214

4 — *Methods of Private Religious Living,* p. 58 (Macmillan Company)

5 — The Mystery, in *Hermione and Other Poems* (Houghton Mifflin Company)

6 — *Letters of John Keats,* edited by SIDNEY COLVIN, p. 43 (Macmillan Company)

7 — A Free Man's Worship, in *Mysticism and Logic,* p. 56 (W. W. Norton Company, Inc.)

8 — *The Enduring Quest,* by H. A. Overstreet, p. 264 (W. W. Norton Company)

9 — *Letters of Emily Dickinson,* edited by Todd, p. 286

10 — *De diversis quaestionibus octaginta tribus,* XXXV, 2

11 — *Men and Memories,* by W. Rothenstein, Vol. I, p. 32 (Faber and Faber, Ltd.)

12 — *Confessions,* Book VII, Chap. X

13 — *The Stromata,* Book VII, Chap. VII, 42: 3

14 — Quoted in W. Herrmann's *Communion with God,* Eng. tr., p. 159

15 — Quoted in *Prayer,* by F. Heiler, Eng. tr., p. 272 (Oxford University Press)

16 — Isaiah 64: 7

17 — *Ante-Nicene Fathers,* Vol. VIII, p. 781

18 — *William Graham Sumner,* by Harris E. Starr, p. 543 (Henry Holt and Company)

19 — *Nathaniel Hawthorne,* by George E. Woodberry, p. 184 (Houghton Mifflin Company)

20 — *The Testing of Diana Mallory,* p. 292 (Harper and Brothers)

CHAPTER IV

1 — *An Idealist View of Life,* by S. Radhakrishnan, the Hibbert Lectures for 1929, p. 27 (George Allen and Unwin, Ltd.)

2 — This point of view is pled for by FRANK LENWOOD in *Jesus—Lord or Leader?* (Constable and Company, Ltd.)

3 — Plato's *Republic,* Book II, 383

4 — *Les Miserables,* Part I, Book VII, Chap. XI

5 — *What I Owe to Christ,* p. 352 (The Abingdon Press)

6 — *On the Veiling of Virgins,* Chap. I, *Ante-Nicene Fathers,* Vol. IV, p. 27

7 — *Marius the Epicurean,* Chap. XIV (Macmillan Company)

8 — *The Social Teaching of the Christian Churches,* by ERNST TROELTSCH, Eng. trans., Vol. II, p. 1013

9 — *Stormers of Heaven,* by SOLOMON B. FREEHOF, pp. 210, 211 (Harper and Brothers)

CHAPTER V

1 — Exodus 31: 2-5

2 — *The Life and Letters of Sir Edmund Gosse,* by EVANS CHARTERIS, p. 10 (Harper and Brothers)

3 — *Charles Darwin,* Autobiography and Letters, p. 101 (D. Appleton and Company)

4 — Address on his seventieth birthday, in *Vortrage und Reden,* Vol. I, pp. 15, 16

5 — In the Introduction to *The Fortunes of Nigel*

6 — In De Finibus, in *Roundabout Papers*

7 — *George Eliot's Life,* by J. W. Cross, Vol. III, p. 424 (W. Blackwood and Sons)

8 — *Life of Robert Louis Stevenson,* by Graham Balfour, Vol. II, pp. 19, 20 (Charles Scribner's Sons)

9 — *Adam Bede,* Chapter IV

10 — *Reminiscences,* edited by J. A. Froude, p. 52 (Charles Scribner's Sons)

11 — *Incompatibility in Marriage,* by Felix Adler, p. 15 (D. Appleton and Company)

12 — *The Spirit of World Politics,* by William Ernest Hocking, p. 165 (Macmillan Company)

CHAPTER VI

1 — *Christiana Religionis Institutio,* Book I, Chap. XIII, 1 and 21

2 — *The Laws of Ecclesiastical Polity,* Book I, Chap. II, 2

3 — *The Hunting of the Snark,* by Lewis Carroll

4 — *An Idealist View of Life,* by S. Radhakrishnan, p. 59 (George Allen and Unwin, Ltd.)

5 — *Beauty,* by John W. Cross, in the *Yale Review* for April, 1922

6 — *Prelude,* Book I

7 — *The Forsyte Saga,* by John Galsworthy, p. 504 (Charles Scribner's Sons)

8 — Clement, *Stromata,* Book II, Chap. V

9 — *The Letters of George Meredith,* Vol. I, pp. 165, 166 (Charles Scribner's Sons)

10 — Augustine, *Confessions,* Book VII, Chaps. XVII and XVIII

11 — *History of Dogma,* by Adolf Harnack, Eng. tr., Vol. VII, p. 199

12 — Shelley, *Adonais,* liv

13 — *The Direct and Fundamental Proofs of the Christian Religion,* by George William Knox, p. 149 (Charles Scribner's Sons)

14 — Mrs. Browning, *Aurora Leigh,* Fourth Book

15 — Henry W. Longfellow, *The Sound of the Sea*

16 — *The Riddle of the New Testament,* by Sir Edwyn Hoskins and Noel Davey, p. 255 (Harcourt, Brace and Company)

17 — *The Birth and Growth of Religion,* by George Foot Moore, p. 178 (Charles Scribner's Sons)

18 — *A History of the Reformation,* by T. M. Lindsay, Vol. I, pp. 471, 472 (Charles Scribner's Sons)

19 — *De Trinitate,* v, 10

20 — George Matheson, from the hymn "Gather them in, Thou Love that fillest all"

21 — *History of Dogma,* by Adolf Harnack, Eng. tr., Vol. VII, p. 199

22 — *Ibid.,* Vol. VII, p. 274